WEST SLOPE COMMUNITY LIBRARY
(503) 292-6416
MEMBER OF
WASHINGTON COUNTY COOPERATIVE
LIBRARY SERVICES

A Life Less
Throwaway

D0012802

WEST SLOPE COMMUNITY LIBRARY
(503) 292-6416
MEMBER OF
WASHINGTON COUNTY COOPERATIVE
LIBRARY SERVICES

A Life Less Throwaway

The Lost Art of Buying for Life

Tara Button

TEN SPEED PRESS
California | New York

For my great makers:
My parents, who made me,
Mark, the one making dreams come true,
Juliet, the best maid of honor,
and Howard, who makes me happy every day

Contents

Introduction

or

Why I Want My Grandmother's Tights

My grandmother's tights used to last forever. They were so strong, people could tow cars with them, and did! Granny got two pairs—one to wash and one to wear. But then, the manufacturers decided to change the way their stockings were made, and not for the better. So today, when *I* reach for a pair of tights, it's like playing panty hose roulette. Which pair will tear this morning?

It may not seem like a crisis to have a drawer stuffed with compromised hosiery, but I see it as a very small glimpse into a much larger problem. Our houses, our whole *lives*, have become stuffed full of things that let us down, causing our stress levels to skyrocket and our bank accounts to empty. But it's precisely *because* these things are poorly made, or just a fad, that we are perversely compelled to buy more of them.

But couldn't life be different? What if we decided to surround ourselves with beautiful, well-made objects that lasted forever, instead of "for now" things that soon need replacing?

That was the seed of an idea that came to me in 2013. Before then, I was a dues-paying, card-carrying member of the impulse-shopper club who never questioned the things I bought. I'd always been a spendthrift; my mother says that as a child it never much mattered how much pocket money I was given, I was always broke. And this behavior carried on into adulthood. Once I'd decided I wanted something, I "needed" it *right away*, and so my life and home became filled with stuff that was "almost but not quite right." Longevity wasn't one of my criteria, so I owned temporary things, poorly thought-through and soon-regretted clothes or hobby and fitness equipment bought in fits of short-lived enthusiasm.

My habitual impulse-buying eventually led to excessive credit-card debt, leaving me feeling out of control, childish, and angry with myself. I would come home to a chronically cluttered house, which was exhausting to tidy or clean, and stare blankly at my piles of fast-fashion clothes, wondering why I felt I had nothing to wear.

Like many people, I was stumbling through life believing that "when this happens or when I have that, *then* I'll be happy." Without a clear sense of self, I'd unconsciously mold my character into whatever I thought my partners wanted me to be. When my last relationship failed, therefore, I felt so lost, I had to spend some time on antidepressants. With my thirties looming, I felt as though I'd screwed up my life and chucked it away like a used tissue.

At the same time, I'd managed to fall into the moral wasteland that is the advertising world. My job was now to write ads for some of the world's biggest brands, trying to persuade people like me to buy more stuff, whether they needed it or not. A few years ago, while on vacation, I had a full-on breakdown in front of my friends; and in the plane restroom on the way home, I looked in the mirror and vowed to make a change. I just wasn't sure what that change would be.

The change came in the form of a pot—a baby-blue Le Creuset Dutch oven given to me for my thirtieth birthday. It came with a reputation for lasting for generations, and when I held it, it just *felt* like an heirloom. It was startlingly beautiful, and I reflected that owning it meant I potentially never had to buy another one again. "If only everything in my life were like this," I thought.

Enthused, I set out to find more objects that I would never have to replace—objects that would work with me and grow old with me; beautiful, classic objects worth committing to and taking care of.

I assumed there'd be a website that sold a collection of lifetime products, but when I went looking for one, it didn't exist. "Maybe I could be the one to build it," I dared to think.

I had zero web-design skills, but the more I thought about it, the more powerful the idea seemed. If this website could release people from the constant pressure to renew and replace, it might solve some of the biggest problems the world was facing. It would ease the clutter, unhappiness, and debt that came with overconsumption; lessen the environmental impact of our throwaway society; and save us all money in the long term.

I started to make changes in my own life and uncovered the surprising practical and emotional benefits that come with choosing to bring only those objects into your life that reflect your values and will be with you for decades to come.

I knew that if I didn't at least try to build the website, I'd always regret it. So in 2015, I started BuyMeOnce.com, and began hunting for lifetime items in my spare time. I cut my salary in half and lived on minimum wage so I could split my time between my day job and building my business.

Painfully slowly, and after several false starts, the site started to come together. It was very basic and had no means of making money, and I had no idea if anyone would ever visit it. Most likely, I thought, it would remain a lonely result on the sixth page of a Google search.

Then, in 2016, miraculously and quite unexpectedly, the world found it. The site went viral, thousands of e-mails flooded in, BuyMeOnce was featured in almost every major newspaper in the United Kingdom and I was suddenly being asked to be on TV in America. I hadn't realized it, but I had tapped into something that people all around the world were feeling. They were tired of our throwaway culture.

By this stage, my life had completely turned around. My spending was under control because I was living by my newfound philosophy. Sadly, I hadn't morphed into a "naturally" tidy person, but after giving away more than half my wardrobe and countless boxes of clutter, any mess I made was easily dealt with in a couple of minutes. Owning items I loved for the long term also meant I naturally started caring for them better and lost things less frequently. I'd also stopped worrying about keeping up with the Joneses, and reconnected with the person I really was. This, together with doing something I truly believed in, had raised my self-worth and allowed me to enter into a relationship based on a joyful connection rather than neediness. I had found my best friend, and now husband—a kind, funny, bespectacled man who makes me happier than I had imagined possible.

I now have the opportunity to share with you what I believe is a life-enhancing way of thinking and behaving. My hope is that this book can be helpful on a personal level and, if it falls into the hands of enough people, helpful to the planet.

WHAT CAN ONE LITTLE BOOK DO?

This book tells the story of how we've sleepwalked into a world where our lives are focused on a constant churn of items with little lasting value.

I'll also reveal how we're manipulated to feel that our current possessions (and, by extension, ourselves) are inadequate, and how this drives us to constantly upgrade our wardrobes, homes, and technology. After ten years in the advertising world, I'm able to take you behind ad-land's glitzy curtain to reveal the tricks of the trade and arm you against its devious tactics.

Overbuying habits are often linked to low self-worth, so this book also contains sections to help you to value yourself. No object can make you more or less of a person. Once you've truly understood that possessions don't have such power, you're able to choose, with much greater ease, which ones to bring into your life. "A life less throwaway" becomes simultaneously a simpler *and* richer life, because the focus is off consumption and on what really matters.

As my company name, BuyMeOnce, suggests, living a life less throwaway *does* involve buying certain things, but this lifestyle isn't about buying beautiful stuff to gloat over, it's about buying only those items that will support a functioning and fulfilling life.

MINDFUL CURATION

I call my method "mindful curation," which might sound as pretentious as bringing your own tablecloth to KFC but is the best term for it. It is "mindful" because it is done with purpose and thought. And it is "curation" because, like a curator putting together a collection in an art gallery, it's about picking only those things that will work together to form a home and a life that uniquely reflects you and your needs. It can be broken down into ten steps.

1. Understand the pressures that promote mindless buying and then develop tactics to free yourself from them (*Chapters 2 to 6 and 10*).

2. Investigate your life's purpose and the long-term priorities that will help you meet this purpose (*Chapter 7*).

3. Identify which items you need to fulfill those priorities and to live comfortably without being swayed by status (*Chapters 7 to 9*).

4. Identify your true tastes and sense of style so you can buy future-proof items (*Chapters 2 and 5*).

5. Identify your values and the brands that reflect those values (*Chapter 7*).

6. Take stock of the items you already have in order to understand your present tastes, priorities, and buying habits (*Chapter 8*).

7. Let go of the clutter and the superfluous (*Chapter 8*).

8. Develop a healthy attitude toward money (*Chapter 15*).

9. Choose each new item with your long-term priorities and tastes in mind (*Chapters 5, 10, and 11*).

10. Develop the skills to take care of and keep the things you've chosen to bring into your life (*Chapter 12*).

This book contains practical exercises on how to put these steps into action. Skipping straight to them may leave you with a shallower understanding of why they are important. However, if time is short and you just want to get cracking, go ahead—there's a list on the next page, or simply flip through the book. You'll find every exercise has a square ❏ at the top corner of the page. Ticking off this box after completing an exercise will give you a burst of happy chemicals, keeping you motivated and confident—so use these boxes!

This is, above all, a book on how to be happy in our ultracommercial world. Please use it in the way that's most helpful to you.

Let's get started!

List of Exercises

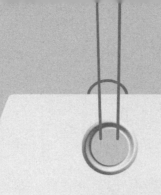

PART 1

Broken Behavior

1

Mindful Curation

or
How to Resist a World That's Trying to Make Us Broke and Lonely

Our relationship with "stuff" may sit squarely at the center of this book but I should be clear from the outset that my purpose isn't to make you obsess over material things. In fact, it's to help you do the opposite. I want to give you the tools to understand what you need and don't need, and how to make the objects in your life work for you in the long term.

THE BENEFITS OF MINDFUL CURATION

We have only a limited amount of money, headspace, and time to spend as we frolic on this planet, and we can very easily waste a huge amount of each on meaningless stuff. Mindful curation helps us to free up all three, so that we can utilize them enjoying the things we find most meaningful.

Being more mindful about what we buy protects us from impulse spending and gives us more resilience to advertising and marketing manipulation. And we find that we start saving money over time. Crucially, though, it doesn't feel as if we're making a sacrifice. Savings come naturally out of a better understanding of what we need and what best serves us, which is usually much less than the average person buys.

When we practice mindful curation, we're releasing ourselves from the trivial, the bland, and the shoddy, and living a life where the objects around us perfectly match our needs, pull their weight, reflect our values, and put a smile on our face. This frees our time and energy for the things that matter most, like family, friends, pursuing our passions, and finally finding out who wins *Game of Thrones*.

THE BENEFITS OF LONGER-LASTING PRODUCTS

Not all products are made equal, and I believe we've left longevity out of our decision-making for far too long. The commercial world does everything it can to tempt us away from longevity, but that only serves its ever-hungry self, not us, the people who have to deal with the broken zippers, rattling washing machines, and rips in the crotches of our jeans.

When I started buying for a lifetime, it forced me to think far more deeply about what I wanted that lifetime to look like. This meant that the possessions I "curated" automatically started to reflect the deeper and more stable elements of my character, values, and personal style. This has brought a lovely natural harmony to my home, creating an atmosphere in which I feel refreshed and calm because it is authentically "me."

My home had previously been a stressful one. Every time I walked through my little kingdom and saw the toaster that wouldn't pop, the wonky flat-pack drawers, dried-up pens, and unreliable dishwasher, I'd feel anxiety rise up. Once I started surrounding myself with objects I could trust, my home became a much more relaxing and nurturing place to be.

Another delightful side effect of buying fewer things and not replacing your items so regularly is that you can afford to buy higher-quality, better-crafted products, so your quality of life can actually feel higher.

IS IT MINIMALISM?

Mindful curation definitely has its roots in the minimalist movement. However, while minimalism tends to be quite clear on what we should cut out of our lives (as much as possible), it can leave us hanging when it comes to deciding what to bring into them and how to bypass the pressures to buy more than we need.

With mindful curation, we aren't trying to reduce our possessions down to a magic number of objects or compete to see who can live with the least. Instead, we're finding out much more about ourselves and our values and using that knowledge as a shield against clutter and the tricks and temptations of marketers. So, with mindful curation you end up owning exactly the right amount for you—no more and no less—and this will be different for everyone.

MINDFUL CURATION VERSUS MINDLESS CONSUMPTION

"The best things in life aren't things."
—ART BUCHWALD

Mindful curation is a simple idea, but it can be challenging at first because there are so many forces trying to get us to think in the opposite way—the way of "mindless consumption."

Mindless consumption sounds free-spirited and potentially quite fun. It's the unwritten hashtag for every photo uploaded by the "Rich Kids of Instagram," the hidden subtitle on every "haul video." The danger of mindless consumption though is that it makes us morbidly materialistic, meaning that a huge amount of our attention is focused on our wealth, our stuff, and our status. And materialistic people have been shown to be (deep breath) less generous, less agreeable, less healthy, less likely to help others, less satisfied with their lives, less satisfied with their jobs, less caring about the environment, more likely to gamble, more likely to be in debt, lonelier, worse at keeping friends, and less close to the friends they do have. Oh, and materialistic kids do less well at school.[1]

In short—it's really bad!

Yet advertisers, the government, our friends, and even our kids surround us with messages and put constant pressure on us to focus on materialistic things. On top of this, on average we see more than 5,000 marketing messages a day.[2]

Unsurprisingly, this takes its toll. Research shows that briefly subjecting someone to photos of luxury objects or even just words such as *status* or *expensive* can trigger a more depressed mood, feelings of wanting to outdo others, and less willingness to socialize.[3] Tim Kasser, who has been studying the effects of materialism for almost two decades, describes the impact as a see-saw effect. When we see ourselves as "consumers" rather than "people" (which is easily triggered through marketing messaging) we focus more on materialistic urges, such as our status and competitiveness. This causes an upswing of negative materialistic thoughts and a downswing of positive urges toward community, connection, generosity, trust, and cooperation—all the things that have been proven to make our lives more fulfilling and happy.

So, when your granddad says that people were nicer in the "good ol' days," in this aspect, it's true. Our materialistic tendencies have increased so much in the last few decades that our sense of community, our trust in others, and our ability to be happy have been gravely reduced.

It's a dangerous spiral. A study of 2,500 Americans over six years concluded that no matter how much money you possessed to spend, materialism was linked to an increase in loneliness, and loneliness in turn increased materialism.[4] In the 1970s and '80s, 11 to 20 percent of Americans reported that they often felt lonely; in 2010, that figure rose to between 40 and 45 percent.[5]

How does materialism make us lonelier? The messages we see in ads and social media channels perpetuate a myth that having things or looking a certain way makes us worthy of love and admiration. It's very natural to want to feel special and appreciated, so we start to focus on our looks and achievements and buy high-status items that others will admire. However, any admiration or connection we gain is on a shallow level, and because it isn't based on anything authentic, it leaves us feeling disconnected and unsatisfied. So we try even harder to get the love we need by showing the world our possessions, our status, and our achievements, never guessing that the constant focus on the self means that the connection to others, the connection that we need to be happy, isn't going to happen.

WHY IS THIS IMPORTANT NOW?

I'm not going to spend too much time pressing the environmental point, because I think we all know that mindless consumerism is pushing our poor planet to a crisis point. We need to save it, and dropping the ball isn't really an option. We live on the ball, and we don't have another one to move to.

At the same time, sadly, materialism and narcissism are on the rise. A study published in 2012 tracked the values of graduates since 1966 and found that the importance given to status, money, and narcissistic life goals, such as "being famous," had risen significantly, whereas the importance given to finding meaning and purpose in life and a desire to help others had fallen.[6] In addition, a study of students over the last thirty years has found that college kids today are about 40 percent lower in empathy than the students of twenty or thirty years ago.[7]

We have become "all about me" rather than "all about we." The irony is that self-focused people hurt themselves more than anyone else. I don't feel that it is a coincidence that the use of anti-depressants has gone up 400 percent in the United States in the last decade.[8]

We are at a crisis point for people and planet. The hour is late, but there's still time to turn things around.

IS OUR STUFF GETTING IN THE WAY OF WHAT'S IMPORTANT?

In 2010, five Pacific Islanders who had lived all their lives with practically no possessions were flown to the United Kingdom to be part of a TV program where they looked at modern life.[9] As they walked around their host's house and explored London, they were surprised by all the "useless extra things" they saw, saddened that busy commuters wouldn't stop and talk to them, and shocked at seeing homeless people. This would "never be allowed to happen" in their community.

The tribesmen's material-free lives meant that they hadn't lost sight of what was important: love, respect, and enjoying each other's company. When they first arrived, they were all given their own rooms in their host's big house. Later, when they stayed at a more modest place and all five of them were put together in a small bedroom, they declared themselves happier because now they were "able to talk to each other."

It's easy to romanticize the "noble savage" life. There are of course many downsides, including lack of healthcare, gender equality, and Ben & Jerry's, but it is interesting to explore how our own society's values might change if materialism were reduced.

In 2016, my then fiancé, Howard, and I were invited to be on a TV show trying to discover this very thing. Six participants were stripped bare of all their possessions. Literally. Crouching-beneath-your-window-sill-so-the-neighbors-don't-see-your-dangly-bits bare. All their stuff was locked away in a nearby shed and each day they were able to choose one possession that they most wanted to have back in their lives. Howard is not a naked person, so *Life Stripped Bare* went on to be made without us.[10]

One of the brave volunteers, Heidi, a pink-haired fashion designer with thirty-one bikinis, sobbed as the removal vans arrived. "My stuff defines me," she said. "I want people to like me, think I'm cool, think I'm nice, and if I don't have my hipster coat or my rings on, I don't think they will like me."

On Day 2, after a grueling night on the floor, she reflected, "Yesterday I was crying because I wanted everything. Today I just want my mattress." In fact, she got more than that. Out on the street, two passing girls stopped to help her carry the mattress and they bonded over the funny situation. Almost in tears, Heidi said to the camera, "Now that I've got some friends, I honestly feel I've got everything. . . . When you have nothing, people make the whole world of difference."

I'd like to turn this on its head and say, "When you've got people, there's nothing much else you need in the world." All the participants of *Life Stripped Bare* found that once their basic comfort levels were met, they became less and less bothered about picking up new items from the shed. We can be happy with very little, yet, due to materialism, the average home has 300,000 items in it.

So how can we reverse this trend? Let's start with some exercises to break free of materialism.

PERSUADE YOURSELF OF THE IMPORTANCE OF NON-MATERIAL ACTIONS

You may think you don't need persuading that there's more to life than materialism, especially after reading this chapter, but write an e-mail to yourself about it anyway. This may seem a bit twee, but has been proven by professor and clinical psychologist Natasha Lekes to have a tangible impact on your happiness.[11] I'll even start you off.

Dear me,
This feels odd but I'm going to tell you about why I think having good relationships, helping the world to be a better place, and growing as a person are so important . . .

SIGN UP FOR BUYMEONCE MANTRAS

Sign yourself up for free daily mantras at BuyMeOnce.com. These short phrases will help your subconscious make good choices for you and you'll be less swayed by materialistic messaging. Here are three to get you going.

- I am good enough.

- I have everything I need to be happy.

- I am grateful for all I have.

SIMPLE WAYS TO COMBAT MATERIALISM EVERY DAY

- Remind yourself upon waking that this life is amazing but also short—smile and say "thank you for the day."

- Find time each day to focus on your own personal growth and self-worth. (You'll find ideas in this book.)

- Find people who share your passions and build a sense of community with them.

- Block materialistic messages as much as possible (more on this later).

- Practice meditation and mindfulness—there's a wealth of material out there to get you started.

- Feeling close to nature has been shown to decrease materialism, so get out as much as possible, even if you just go into your backyard or a public park. Nature documentaries can also be a lovely way to escape from seeing "stuff."

2

Planned Obsolescence

or

Why They Don't Make 'em Like They Used To

"Obsolescence" is a horrible mouthful of a word that essentially means "when something becomes useless." "Planned obsolescence," therefore, is when people plan for our products to become useless. Deliberately. Let that sink in for a second.

There are two main ways planned obsolescence happens. The first is physical obsolescence, where companies actually design products to break before they need to. The other is psychological obsolescence, where people are made to feel that they no longer want the possessions they already have. The use of both has exploded in the last century, with companies conspiring to change the way we shop forever.

Planned obsolescence was born (and raised to be very naughty) in America. In the 1930s, when Europeans were still making their possessions last as long as possible, industrial designers in the United States justified all the new waste caused by obsolescence by pointing out that, while Europe had used up many of its natural resources, "in America, we still have tree-covered slopes to deforest and subterranean lakes of oil to tap."[1] Some people did take the concerns about extra waste and environmental damage seriously, but their concerns were quickly brushed under the cheap new rugs that were being made. At this time, America had a problem with overproduction. By the Great Depression, the States had gotten very good at making lots of things very quickly, but less good at selling them.

In 1932, a Russian American named Bernard London published a grand plan entitled "Ending the Depression Through Planned Obsolescence." After noticing that people held on to their products longer in an economic depression, which meant less money being spent on goods, he suggested that every product, from shoes to cars, houses to hats, be given a set lifespan. Once that lifespan was up, the items would be declared legally "dead" and people would have to turn them in to the government to be destroyed or risk a fine. They would then, of course, have to buy them again new.[2] This particular scheme never came about. Maybe because the government realized that forcing people to hand over their possessions for incineration was a sure-fire way to get unelected.

What ended up happening was stealthier. Businessmen, politicians, manufacturers, and the advertising industry colluded to change both products and minds, with the aim of turning citizens into consumers. In fact, they had been colluding already.

THE LIGHT BULB CONSPIRACY

The most famous proven case of planned obsolescence was the subject of a truly shocking documentary called *The Light Bulb Conspiracy*.[3] It's famous because it's one of the few times actual written proof has been found that this shady practice takes place.

By 1924, light bulbs had been getting better in quality for some time; some were now lasting up to 2,500 hours. Then, representatives of the biggest electric companies in the world, including Osram, Philips, and General Electric, met in Geneva on Christmas Eve to hatch a very un-Christmassy plan.

By the end of the meeting in a cramped back room, they had formed a secret group known as the Phoebus Cartel, and had all agreed to regularly send their bulbs to Switzerland to be tested to ensure the bulbs broke within 1,000 hours. They even agreed to be fined for every hour that went over the limit.

If you look at the following graph showing how long bulbs last, you'll see that there's a steady decline until the cartel reached their goal and the average bulb expectancy ground out at around 1,025 hours.

How did they get away with it? Many of the changes were sold to consumers as efficiencies and improvements in brightness. And despite lasting less than half as long as the older light bulbs, the new ones were often even more expensive.

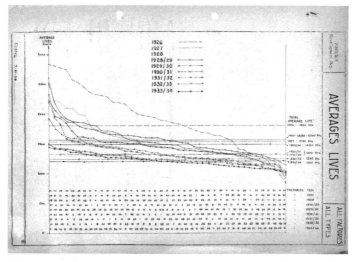

Photo: Landesarchiv Berlin

The companies profited enormously from their tactics; one reported that their sales had increased fivefold since they changed their designs to be more delicate.

The cartel was disbanded during the Second World War when it became a little awkward for German, British, and American businessmen to get together. But the damage had been done; the life expectancy of bulbs didn't recover.

I recently had the pleasure of talking to several people who work in the light-bulb industry today. When I shared the story of the 1924 Phoebus Cartel, they said that in many ways things were no better now.

One engineer told me that one of the most underhanded tactics she'd witnessed recently was bulbs being sold with an advertised life of seven years but purposefully designed so they would last two or three years, just long enough to avoid customer complaints and returns. And this company was a major player in the light-bulb world. "The light-bulb industry is full of misinformation, and I've run independent tests on bulbs," she said. "Some of them run so hot there's no way the components inside will survive the time the packaging says they will."

"They're lying to us. There are all sorts of cheats going on. For example, you get guarantees that are only valid if the bulb is used for one to two hours per day." And this just isn't how bulbs are used.

Beyond bulbs

By the 1950s, obsolescence was fully grown and had left home to travel the world. Now its influence can be seen everywhere, from the furniture dumped outside homes in Europe to the mountains of electrical waste in Asia.

In the 1970s, '80s, and '90s, voices started being raised about the need for products to last longer to avoid an environmental crisis, but governments and businesses chose instead to concentrate their efforts on recycling.

Recycling is a positive thing and certainly takes away the guilt we feel about discarding something. But the truth is, the environmental difference between being able to keep using something and recycling it is colossal. Recycling still takes energy, waste collection, and processing, and usually requires manufacturing a new object to replace the one we are discarding. This suits companies very well, but we and our planet end up paying the price.

So here we are. The calls for longer-lasting products have been ignored for decades, planned obsolescence reigns supreme, and the commercial world is steering us, blindfolded, into an iceberg of trash. But we do have an opportunity to turn this around. Here are the main forms of physical obsolescence and what we can do to combat it.

QUALITY STRIPPING

We've all experienced quality stripping, and I'm not talking about particularly adept G-string jiggling. I've been told by several engineers that it isn't necessarily that they are purposefully building products to break, but that every year they might be asked to take more costs out of the product, so the materials get thinner and cheaper and the quality starts to come down. Quality stripping is done to products all over the world, all of the time, and it's not even being denied, it's just being explained away.

There is solid evidence that appliances are breaking earlier and earlier. In fact, the number of appliances that must be replaced because of breakage has doubled since 2004. Most shocking, boilers that lasted a wonderful 23 years in 1980 are expected to last only 12 years by 2020.[4]

Also, while most engineers are craftsmen and generally want to make the highest-quality products they can, many businesspeople see manufacturing companies purely as money-making projects. Whether they make hair dryers or hamburgers makes no difference to them. One scene from *The Light Bulb Conspiracy* that filled me with dread was footage of a teacher in a design course handing out various products to his students and asking them how long they thought each was designed to last. "It's important for you to know," he said, "because you'll have to design to a certain lifespan and to the business model the company wants." This is particularly disheartening, as he's teaching the next generation of designers not to make the best products they can, but ones that last as long as they need to for the company to sell them.

"Companies have become increasingly greedy for a quick buck, and short-term greed produces massive problems," explains Thor Johnsen, who has been in the business of buying, selling, and managing other companies for many years. "Companies today put nearly all their money into branding and marketing, spend a bit on design, and then build their products as cheaply as possible. That's the model now."

"Why are they getting away with it?" I asked.

"The trouble is," Thor responded, "shoppers might say they want quality when we ask them, but when we watch them, they don't actually buy for quality. They buy for convenience or price."

"Do you think part of the trouble," I suggested, "is that people go into a shop and see a row of products and can only guess which one lasts the longest? So they end up going for what's cheapest or what goes best with their kitchen."

"Yeah, that might be it," he said. "Branding used to help us know which was the best quality. But that's just not the case anymore."

So far, so depressing. And this isn't the end of the bad news. With so many products now being made overseas, there is a temptation for factories to secretly change the quality of the products after the first couple of batches. The factories win the business by making something great, but then start cutting corners. Or everything but the corners, producing shoddy products that quickly end up in the trash.

This isn't just annoying and wasteful but also sometimes downright dangerous. Tires might be made with cheaper-quality rubber that explodes at high speeds, or the paint used on toys might be switched for a cheaper toxic lead variety. We're often left at the mercy of unscrupulous manufacturers, who are happy to take our money and give us poison and trash in exchange. Unfortunately getting some factories to take responsibility is almost impossible.

If you're reading this and thinking it's as depressing as an empty toilet-roll holder, I apologize. It is depressing, but it's also important to know what we're up against, so we can know how to combat it. There's a section coming up on how to do just that.

MAKING IT UNFIXABLE— OBSOLESCENCE IN DISGUISE

One scorching August day in 2016, I invited my friend Tom Lawton over to look at toasters. Tom is a rather bizarre combination of engineer, inventor, and TV presenter, and I gave him the challenge of looking into how six different toaster brands were made and how that might affect their longevity.

"What we're looking for," Tom said, "is the weakest link. A product is only as good as its worst flaw."

We looked at the toasters to get an insight into the choices that engineers had made: the materials used, how a product is put together, and areas where the durability is being compromised. One of the things that immediately jumped out at us, though, was how hard these toasters were to get into. Some even had special star-shaped security screws. One did come apart eventually, exposing a jagged metal edge that cut open Tom's hand. These toasters were clearly designed to be put together cheaply, not to be taken apart and fixed.

Some manufacturers do this to protect themselves. If a consumer fixes a product and it goes wrong, it can be a public relations disaster for the brand, so you can see where this defensive thinking comes from. At the same time, being sold products that are designed to be unfixable (even by a trained engineer like Tom) has conditioned us to feel helpless when things break. So when their weakest link fails they are seen as "dead" and destined for the big scrap heap in the sky (or sea . . . or slum).

Smartphones are perhaps the most notorious for this. Their weakest link is their battery, and the makers know it, but some of the brands make it impossible or prohibitively expensive for people to replace the battery. When it goes, often the whole phone goes. There's been some backlash over this, but in general we've rolled over and accepted the situation. Perhaps seduced by having an excuse to buy the newest model?

But by preventing us from replacing the battery, the manufacturers are limiting the whole phone's life to the life of the battery. Imagine your car tires wearing out and the manufacturer telling you that you might as well buy a whole new car. This is essentially what many technology companies are doing right now.

Phones aren't the only products that have come under fire recently either. A 2015 investigation into washing machines showed their design had changed over time "and not for the better." Now manufacturers are sealing the drums inside, meaning that if the bearings go (one of the top five reasons for a breakdown) we have to replace the entire drum, which may cost almost as much as a new machine. If the machine's out of warranty, we'll generally be told it's not worth fixing and we should buy a new one.[5]

When asked why they now sealed in the drums, manufacturers claimed it made the machines more reliable. However, the most reliable brand, Miele, doesn't seal its drums, so this excuse feels as suspicious to me as finding a feather in my cat's bed.

It's obvious something nasty has happened. Clearly, planned obsolescence isn't as simple as mysterious people in white coats putting mythical "kill chips" in our blenders to stop them from working the day after the warranty expires. It's subtler and more insidious. Still, I believe it can be overcome and we can drastically improve the quality of what we are sold if we employ some of the following tactics. The fight back begins here.

What to do?

The emotional and financial toll of having something break on you is rarely thought about, but whenever a vital product falls apart it brings an added level of stress into your life. It can even trap low-income families into a cycle of poverty, forcing them to pay out again and again for shoddy appliances. Some might say that it is the duty of businesspeople to put profits first; however, as I sit here writing this, I would argue that to put profits before people and planet is dangerous, short-sighted, selfish, and just plain rude. Fortunately, as consumers, we do have some power if we know how to use it.

When they build it to break

- Get angry and demand more. According to a report on product durability, when it comes to small appliances, we're upset if something lasts less than three years and satisfied if it lasts 7.7 years.[6] I think we should expect better. If something has a simple function, like to boil water or toast bread, there's no excuse for it not to last decades. The fact that we're happy with less is worrying—we've been trained to expect poor longevity.

- Look out for petitions to change the laws.

- France already has a law to prevent planned obsolescence, and a director of any company caught in "built to break" tactics can now go to jail for two years and face a fine of up to 5 percent of the company's revenue. I believe this should be the law worldwide, and I'll be fighting to make that happen.

When it breaks

- Let us at BuyMeOnce know. We're aiming to build the biggest database in the world on how long products last.

- Tell the company that you're dissatisfied and then write an online review telling others how long that product lasted for you.

- Support your local fixers who still have the skills to mend things. We need more of these people.

- Try fixing things yourself. (See Appendix I: Care and Repair for advice.)

When buying

- Seek out products that are reviewed independently as lasting longer and those that come with the best warranties.

- Ask a local repairer which models they recommend.

- Buy locally whenever possible to avoid overseas factories with less-rigorous standards.

- Vote for durability with your wallet by buying BuyMeOnce-approved products and we'll soon see more companies upping their game.

- Ask how long a company keeps spare parts and what the most common repair is, and consider buying that part in advance.

When they strip the quality

- Showing companies that you care about longevity is the key to getting it. Ask about it and talk about it on their social media. Be annoying! It's often the best way to make change happen.

- Sign the BuyMeOnce pledge, letting companies know that you'd be willing to support them if they made products that were built to last. This will give them the confidence to change their policies.

- Look at independent reviews to see if the build quality has gone down. You can find these online at CNET, Consumer Reports, the Reddit "Buyitforlife" thread, BuyMeOnce.com, and Amazon. Check the most up-to-date reviews for any evidence of fading quality. The good news is that people tend to be rather vocal when things don't meet the standards they were expecting.

- Support innovative companies that want to do better. If you see a gap in the market, tell BuyMeOnce about it and we'll put it out as a challenge.

- Support the makers and craftspeople who have a real connection to their products. Crowdfunding platforms such as Kickstarter help because they allow makers to go straight to the customer without marketers in between. This means engineers who want to make longer-lasting products can offer them to the public, and if we like the idea, it may well get funded.

When they make their products unfixable

- Vote with your wallet and look for fixable modular versions of products. For example, a Fairphone can be taken apart and upgraded easily.

- If you have a product that needs fixing, visit your local Restart Project or Repair Café, or start your own group through online sites such as Meetup or Facebook. If you haven't repaired a product before, seek an expert's advice first. Some products are perfectly repairable by an average consumer; however, electricity is serious stuff, so do your homework and use parts approved by the manufacturer if possible. (For more on repairs, see Appendix I: Care and Repair.)

THE BUYMEONCE #MAKEITLAST CAMPAIGN

At BuyMeOnce, we're campaigning to get companies to tell us how long they expect their products to last and to make the best products possible. Products, like animals, evolve over time—features that are useful, like a long neck in a giraffe or a long handle on a frying pan to stop burns, should get taken on by the next generation until the design is perfected.

But then money and trends take over. Instead of making the ultimate frying pan, companies concentrate on making the cheapest frying pan. What we end up with is something that will serve as a pan for a few months but soon die. Imagine if the giraffe got the same treatment.

A board meeting at Giraffe-Makers, Inc.

"So we've worked out that halving the length of neck will take costs down by 15 percent per giraffe," says the product developer.

The board members smile and nod to each other.

The head of engineering chimes in nervously, "But then . . . then, it won't be able to eat from the top branches during droughts."

"So?" asks the CEO.

"So it will starve in a year or so . . . as soon as the rains fail." The head of engineering winces.

"Yeah, but . . . it's still a giraffe until then, isn't it? I mean, we can still advertise it as a giraffe, can't we?" The head of marketing lolls her head sardonically to one side and stares at him until he looks away.

"And," points out the CEO, "if they fail earlier, people will just have to buy another one!"

"And we could make them stripy," chimes in the designer. "Stripes are going to be huge next year."

When shoppers were asked what their top motivation was for buying a product, price and style came out on top. Longevity wasn't even on the radar.[7] This is partly because most manufacturers don't want it to be on the radar. If they did, you could be sure that every box would shout about how long you could expect the product inside to last. This is exactly what we're campaigning for at BuyMeOnce. Imagine going to buy an appliance and having a clear idea of how long it would last. It would immediately be obvious which items were the best value over time. Please join us on this mission by signing the #makeitlast petition at change.org or reaching out to us at BuyMeOnce.com.

All these actions can help bring an end to physical obsolescence, but there is something even sneakier going on. While rummaging through our rubbish, a group of academics found that of the household objects thrown away, a whopping 40 percent were still perfectly fuctional![8] So we can't blame all our waste on shoddy product design or irreparability. Something else is also at play here—psychological obsolescence—and it doesn't play fair.

Psychological obsolescence is a technique used by companies to persuade us to replace the products we own, even if they still work perfectly well. Over the last few decades, companies have increasingly conditioned us to see things as temporary and throwaway. They keep us obsessed with the new. They keep us excited, but it is a cheap, short-lived excitement, as the products we adore upon purchase start to shift in our affections. The remainder of this chapter explores the forces that set this in motion and what we can do to combat it.

THE MOTHER OF PSYCHOLOGICAL OBSOLESCENCE

Several men have been given the rather dubious honor of being titled "the father of planned obsolescence," including King Gillette, inventor of the disposable razor; business writer J. Gordon Lippincott; Alfred P. Sloan Jr, president of General Motors, who pioneered the idea of slightly updating the look of cars every year; and General Motors designer Harley J. Earl, who famously said in 1955, "Our job is to hasten obsolescence. In 1934, the average car ownership span was five years; now it is two years. When it is one year, we will have the perfect score."[9] All these men played their part, however, planned obsolescence also has a mother, and she's rather intriguing.

When Christine Frederick was born in 1883, her father apparently cried, "Horrors! Why, it's only a girl!" It wasn't a promising start, but this girl grew up to be energetic, bright, and imposing-looking, even in sepia. She earned a university degree, and public power through her prolific writing and speaking, at a time when most women had neither. Sadly, she then used this rare female freedom to argue that a woman's place was in the home . . . being a consumer. In fact, her 1928 book *Selling Mrs. Consumer* might just as easily have been called *Selling Out Mrs. Consumer*, for part of it was a guide on how companies could manipulate women's insecurities, vanities, and natural feelings of motherly or sexual love to persuade them to consume at an increased rate.

Frederick's main message was that the public should embrace "progressive obsolescence," which involved developing:

> *A state of mind that is highly suggestible and open; eager and willing to take hold of anything new, either in the shape of a new invention or new designs or styles or ways of living.*

> *A readiness to "scrap" or lay aside an article before its natural life of usefulness is completed, in order to make way for the newer and better thing.*

> *A willingness to apply a very large share of one's income, even if it pinches savings, to the acquisition of the new goods or services or way of living.*[10]

In short, she encouraged her readers to become highly suggestible people willing to spend above their means and throw away perfectly useful items—something she called "creative waste." She saw materials as "inexhaustible," and so professed, "There isn't the slightest reason why they should not be creatively 'wasted'" and scoffed at people who bought shoes, clothes, and cars to last as long as possible.

> This is . . . preposterous. If designers and weavers and inventors of rapid machinery make it possible to choose a new pattern of necktie or dress every few weeks, and there is human pleasure in wearing them, why be an old frump and cling to an old necktie or old dress until it wears through?[11]

I suppose in Frederick's mind this brands me and anyone living a life less throwaway as a "preposterous old frump." I wonder if we can get that put on a (lifetime-guaranteed) T-shirt?

MEET THE CONSUMER JONESES

Prior to the twentieth century, people didn't naturally switch their possessions before the goods were worn out, so ever-more reasons had to be invented to get us to change things on a regular basis. Frederick describes how her perfect family, the Consumer Joneses, would behave: immediately embracing new products and updating them twice a year as they got technically better and efficient. This is called the "technical phase." Later, once the technology upgrades have plateaued, they will throw out the old and buy a new product purely for how it looks. This is called the "aesthetic phase."

The technical phase

Frederick makes a valid point in that we do need some people to be willing to take a chance on new technology so that it can progress. Sometimes, new objects come to market that are so good and useful that no one wants the old version. The iPod killed the CD, the CD killed the cassette, and the cassette killed the record for everyone apart from hipsters. It's like a technological survival of the fittest. However, within this, a huge amount of "innovation" is just change for change's sake, and much of the innovation over-complicates products that worked wonderfully in their simplicity. As an engineer friend of mine said, "A toaster doesn't need to be able to do your tax return, it just has to make bread warm and a bit brown on each side." But often, companies will add extra elements to products to justify a higher price tag and to make their product seem new and different from previous models.

My instinct is that most of the time these "innovations" aren't needed. To prove this to myself, I tried to imagine what my life would be like if all consumer product innovation had stopped in the 1930s when Frederick's book came out. Would life be unbearable, or even that different? Not at all. Almost everything in my home would be just as good, if not better, for being made back then. The only things I think I would miss are the kitchen appliances and boiler, the vacuum cleaner, my laptop, phone, electric toothbrush, and car. Around twelve items. That's paltry when you think of all the products that have come out since that decade. How many of them truly do their jobs better?

Sometimes we're sold innovation under the umbrella of "more efficiency." Efficiency is something to strive for, but today we've come to the point where many energy-efficiency improvements in appliances have plateaued, so unless your current model is very old or polluting, it's always better environmentally and financially to hold on to the one you have. The carbon and money you'd save with the more efficient model would be wiped out by the energy and money needed for the new purchase. If you want to buy something new based on efficiency, wait for the great leaps forward that happen less often, such as moving to solar energy.

It's worth questioning our upgrading impulses and thinking through their implications. Technology companies turn to psychological obsolescence to make us upgrade whether the new product is significantly better or not. There's no real reason why Apple should launch new products every year, but mostly we accept this unquestioningly. Start to question it. This is vital, because the lifespans of these products are now shorter than ever, and electrical waste is growing at a scary rate. Eight percent of our household waste is now electronic[12] and 42 million tons of it was generated in 2014.[13] Much of it still works perfectly. It's estimated that if we sold the items instead of trashing them, people in the United States would make around $1 billion.[14] ONE BILLION DOLLARS in the trash! It isn't just that many of these products are toxic once they begin to rot in the ground but also that they have valuable and rare materials still inside them. These are lost to us forever, buried underneath a town's worth of carrot peelings, chicken bones, and poopy diapers.

In one episode of TV series *What to Buy and Why*,[15] my engineer friend Tom Lawton goes to a trash heap and picks out a pair of earphones, a vacuum cleaner, and a mini scooter. Within a couple of minutes, he finds the problems and fixes them easily. The items are worth several hundred dollars. If we could just make a clone army of Toms and set them up fixing the world's electronics, all would be well. One Tom in every town. When I suggested this to him, he laughed and replied, "There used to be—tinkers."

These fixers are becoming rarer, but they do exist, and if we start making the effort to repair rather than replace, there will soon be many more of them. We can also set up petitions and lobby the government to help us repair and reuse. The state runs our recycling facilities because it sees the benefits. There's no reason why it shouldn't run a reuse facility as well. It took time for us to get used to the idea of recycling and it will take us a while to get into the swing of repairing and reusing. But if governments and reuse companies make it simple and easy to do and promote the benefits, then there's no reason why it shouldn't become completely natural to send products off to the repair shop instead of to the junkyard. Sweden has taken some steps by reducing the tax on repairs to try and encourage people to go that route.(For more on repairing, see Chapter 12 and Appendix I.)

Most important, now that we're aware that resources are not, as Christine Frederick described them, "endlessly replenishable," I feel we need to demand that companies, especially tech and appliance companies, start designing products not just to be assembled quickly and cheaply but to be dismantled, repaired, and upgraded quickly and cheaply. This is the dream of a circular economy where nothing is wasted, and the best way to make it happen is to vote with our wallets.

The aesthetic phase

Getting people to discard perfectly working products because they were no longer seen as beautiful was the real masterstroke of psychological obsolescence. Manufacturers started to tweak the look of their offerings every year to make purely useful things fashion items too. These products would then become unfashionable within a few years.

This trend started in car design and quickly moved into home design and appliances. A new model would come out and suddenly people's pride in the old was reduced. It was particularly noticeable in cars, as they were parked on the street, where all the neighbors could see them. The American car was soon considered to be a "kind of motorized magic carpet on which social egos could ascend."[16] Manufacturers might say that the public demanded these constant style changes, but in fact the public had been trained to expect them by the manufacturers themselves. As Charles Kettering, head of research at General Motors, famously wrote, his job was to make people dissatisfied with what they had already.

Interestingly, there was one car company who bucked this trend. The VW Beetle looked exactly the same from 1949 to 1963. In fact, the company ran an advertisement celebrating that fact. Called the "VW Theory of Evolution," it showed rows of identical-looking cars through the years and boasted that the car never changed for change's sake. Volkswagen proved that there was an alternative way for successful companies to behave . . . if they chose to take it. Alas most did not. Frederick might claim not to have encouraged change for change's sake, but this is precisely what happened once the idea of aesthetic psychological obsolescence took hold.

Donald Norman, author of *The Design of Everyday Things*, explains one of the harmful side effects of the aesthetic phase. In essence, designers are under pressure to bring out something that looks different every year, so they never get to perfect their creations and make them the best they can be. They have to start from scratch each time so that something different is seen on the shelves.[17] We can get designers out of this trap by recognizing psychological obsolescence and calling it out when we see it. We should make a distinction between what is genuine progress (switching from a gasoline to an electric car engine) and what is change for change's sake (a car with a slightly wider grill, or "'70s accents"), and shouldn't give up on our products to buy new versions unless there is a compelling reason to do so. A 5 percent–better pillow or coffee machine isn't good enough. If it's 50 to 100 percent better, I might consider it. If it's solving a problem I actually have, I might be interested. Even if the new design is eco-friendlier, in almost all cases (highly polluting cars aside), it's more environmentally sound to stick with what we have for as long as possible.

Fight aesthetic waste by finding your "true taste"

If a designer comes up with a new color scheme or shape that the media or our friends proclaim to be "good taste," is this a good reason to change what we have? I would say it isn't, as taste is in the eye of the taster. You simply can't say someone has "better taste" than someone else. That would be like saying someone's preference for chocolate ice cream is better than someone else's preference for strawberry. Our preferences can change over time, of course, which is why it's important to dig deeper into our true taste when we choose our products in the first place.

As I write this, a decor magazine is urging me to kiss last year's trends of zigzag patterns and brushed metal good-bye and give my home a different look and feel with butterflies and folding furniture. But the new trends they're offering are completely arbitrary and not necessarily a look that resonates with my personal aesthetic. What you choose to bring into your home can have a profound effect on your mood, energy levels, and the time you must spend keeping it in order. Unfortunately, when it comes to buying housewares, psychological obsolescence and impulse buying swing into full force. To counter it, it pays to know your true taste. You may know it already. If not, try the exercise on the next page.

Through my studies into the murky world of obsolescence, I've come to believe that psychological obsolescence is more insidious and dangerous than physical obsolescence, because with the right messaging, marketers can get into your head and make you dislike the things that you liked perfectly well when you bought them. So, if that thought irritates you, read on. Many of the chapters in this book are focused on helping you deal with the lure of psychological obsolescence. We'll start with advertising—the fuel that makes obsolescence run.

IDENTIFYING YOUR HOME DECOR AESTHETIC

This exercise is all about digging down into your true taste. It will take about twenty minutes, so make sure you have enough time.

- Grab a notebook or open a computer document. Make two columns: Like and Dislike.

- Now go online and search for images of interiors. Don't go to an interior magazine but somewhere like Pinterest, Instagram, or Google Images so you can see a mix of pictures from all eras, from the Tudors to the present day.

- Spend the first five minutes just seeing the colors in the pictures, nothing else. Start jotting down what you do and don't like in an interior setting and any color combinations you find pleasing.

- Then spend five minutes on textures and patterns—for example, natural wood, clapboard, granite, or polka dots.

- Now spend five minutes on styling—for example, window shutters and jugs of flowers.

- Spend the last five minutes on types of furniture and appliances—for example, wing chairs, log coffee tables, or retro fridges.

Keep this list handy or go one step further and make a mood board to arm yourself against fads and future-proof your purchases. (For detailed advice on how to find long-lasting home decor, see Chapter 11.)

3

Advertising

or

How Many People Does it Take to Sell a Light Bulb?

According to 1950s industrial designer Brooks Stevens, advertising exists to give people "the desire to own something a little newer, a little better, a little sooner than necessary."[1] Although it's hard to imagine now, we are not naturally rampant consumers. Marketers had to pump this drug of desire into us.

Drawing on my decade working in advertising, this chapter will give you a peek behind the curtain to show you how the Wizards of Ads bamboozle us into spending money we may not have on things we may not really want.

BEHIND THE ADVERTISING CURTAIN

It was a bright day outside, but you'd never have known it. I was sitting on a black fake-leather couch in a vast dark warehouse. The only lights were at the back of the room where the car was waiting for its close-up. This day was the climax of months of preparation. Looking at the scores of stressed-out and scurrying people, it suddenly hit me just how bonkers my job really was; here's how it works.

The car company had hired my agency and we'd done weeks of research into the ominously named "target market," delving deep into the details of how the public thinks, feels, and behaves. Once the agency planners had their strategy, "get people to see the car as a fashion item," they handed it over to me, the "creative." Several weeks and dozens of ideas later, my art director and I had nailed down what we wanted our poster to look like. Then things got practical. I auditioned more than fifty models, looking them up and down to decide whether they had the "right look" to sell a three-door hatchback. Incidentally, having to judge someone else's appearance is not a life-affirming activity. It manages to make you feel disconnected from your humanity, creepy, and fat all at the same time. Despite my final choice being a size 2, the client who sat beside me on the black sofa confided that she was worried the model might be "too chubby." Every detail of the outfit for this not-at-all-chubby woman had been researched, debated, and signed off by multiple people to make sure it hit the target market squarely in the wallet. And clothes stylists, hair and makeup stylists, lighting directors, and photographers and all their many assistants were in overdrive to ensure that both car and model looked *ab-sol-ute-ly* perfect.

Then, photographs began to flash up on a big computer screen where we could examine them, have passionate debates about shoes, and initiate minute changes. Several hours later we congratulated ourselves and went back to the office to pick the final image. Once there, however, none of the shots were considered "just right," so we ended up Photoshopping three different photographs together. Later, expert retouch artists made both the perfect-looking car and the perfect-looking person (who had already been rigorously perfected) look more perfect.

A month later, the poster was finished. It looked, unsurprisingly, rather perfect. It went up on billboards all over the United Kingdom and the whole campaign was considered a success.

Why am I telling you this? It's not to relive my "glory days" in advertising, I promise. It's to show the strategizing and conscious effort behind every tiny detail to create an advertisement that's as seductive as possible. Ads like this are designed to weave a fantasy world around the product and (at a subliminal level) make us want to be, or be with, the people in them. They seduce us by getting bits of our brain that we're not even aware of to think, "I want to look like that. I want to feel like that. I want that life." But the truth is that it's a very cleverly constructed lie. No one looks like that, not even the models in the ads. To look like that, you'd have to pay the fifty or so people at that shoot to construct every split-second of your life and somehow Photoshop you as you walked along the street.

That day, in that room, I had a moment of clarity. Of all the things to spend your life doing, rush around for, lose sleep over, spend hundreds of thousands of dollars on, why *advertising*? What even *is* this?

WHAT EVEN *IS* THIS?
A VERY BRIEF HISTORY OF ADVERTISING

At first, advertising was simply a means of sharing information. One of the first written ads we know of was created 5,500 years ago by a Babylonian guy who inscribed into a clay tablet what cattle and feed his master had for sale. It probably made for dull reading, with no catchy tagline to make the buyers feel better about the prices, but it was an ad.

Before the printing press was invented in the 1400s, town criers gave out the news, sometimes accompanied by a musician, so the first advertising jingle was probably played on a lute! During the 1700s and 1800s, paper "bill" ads were plastered on every public wall available, including cathedrals. These ads became increasingly eye-catching, with varied graphics, fonts, and etchings selling everything from Pears Soap to a recently arrived cargo ship full of "138 Remarkably Healthy Slaves."

In 1941, the first television ad was aired, during a baseball game between the Brooklyn Dodgers and the Philadelphia Phillies. It showed a map of America with a Bulova-branded watch face superimposed over the top. A deep male voiceover announced proudly, "America runs on Bulova time." And that was it. Ad over. If only all advertising breaks were that short. Now, of the five hours that the average person watches TV,[2] approximately 1.2 hours will be ads.[3] This has led me to the terrifying realization that the average American is watching more than three and a half *years* of advertisements over a lifetime! To me, this sounds like the prison sentence you might get for stealing a car, but, in this case, the prison constantly asks for your money and gets irritating songs stuck in your head.

Digital ads are the new town criers, and they don't even play the lute. We now see and hear an estimated 362 ads per day, including more than 5,000 "brand exposures" from logos and other branding devices.[4] It's no wonder that this has greatly affected our behavior. Even if we claim, as many of us do, to "never pay attention to ads," the sheer number of them, coupled with the activity of our ever-curious brains, means their messages sink in somehow, shifting our ideas of what's important and how we feel about things. Rather creepily, there are thousands of people now working on ways of getting more ads in front of us every day. Don't be surprised if in a few years' time, your fridge starts giving you suggestions as to what you might like to fill it with. Mindful curation therefore can't just be about being mindful of the *objects* we allow into our lives but also the messages and content. This doesn't mean a media blackout, but rather that we should aim to identify the sources that nurture us and give us the information we need to make good choices. To everything else we can say, "Thanks, but no thanks."

If we want to stay mindful, we should be on the lookout for anything that sneaks ads into our homes or heads via the back door. Our homes need to be a sanctuary if we are to stay sane in the next millennia. So, in the words of one of my favorite Harry Potter characters, "Constant vigilance!"

THE SEDUCTION OF SYMBOLISM

The biggest change that I've seen in advertising, and something that particularly affects us when we're trying to practice mindful curation, is the switch from useful information that helps us make choices to symbolism and manipulation. You may have noticed that in many ads today, you might not even see the product, just an idea with the brand's logo on it.

For example, Levi's first ads in the 1870s showed two horses trying to rip apart a pair of jeans. The line went "They never rip" and the advertisement went into detail on their quality and construction. In comparison, a 1998 Levi's ad showed a hamster called Kevin running on a wheel to heavy metal music. A little boy speaks over the top:

"Kevin loved his wheel, but one day . . . it broke."

The music stops and the hamster wheel stops working. The light fades in the room as night falls.

"Kevin grew bored . . ."

We see the sun rise and Kevin standing still in the cage. Then a pencil pokes him through the bars and he falls over into his sawdust.

". . . and died."

The "Levi's Original" logo then appears and the ad ends.[5]

The ad caused a flurry of complaints, but what I find interesting is just how far away the ad is from the product it is advertising. A depressed hamster has nothing to do with jeans and yet Levi's wouldn't have paid hundreds of thousands of dollars to run it unless they thought it would increase sales, so what's going on?

What this ad manages to do very well is create a powerful reaction of shocked laughter/disbelief at the same time as we see the Levi's logo. This is classic subliminal messaging. When we next see the Levi's logo, maybe in a store or online, that feeling of heightened activity in our brain will return as an echo in our mind. We probably won't remember the ad, but we will feel a slight thrill—a thrill that will make us far more likely to remember the brand, pay attention to the jeans and buy them. The ad may also be saying that Levi's are for people who love to move or who can't bear to be still and bored. They're for people who want to "live." That is a sentiment that might resonate with many, and it might even make them feel a closeness to the Levi's brand, but it has no basis in the reality of the product.

I believe that this shift from talking about the attributes and quality of a product to the symbolic qualities of a brand goes hand in hand with why the quality of products has fallen. At some point, companies realized they just needed to sell us an *idea*, and if we bought into that idea, we'd probably buy the product too. So they didn't need to put their efforts into making the best products possible, just into making the best ads! Brands who want to change how we feel about their product now change their advertising, instead of changing the product itself. We might think that we're too savvy to be swayed by these strategies, but this is sadly not the case. When my old agency started telling parents that a certain chocolate spread was not just a treat but could be "part of a healthy breakfast," sales doubled!

It is the same with customer service. It's easy to see where brands' priorities lie when they spend $500 billion on marketing and advertising compared to just $9 billion on customer service.[6] Many companies will charm you right up to the moment you've bought their product, and then you'll be invisible to them until they can sell you something that's "even better." In the meantime, what is to be done with their product if it fails is "not their problem."

It is the companies who break this pattern that have the potential to become BuyMeOnce brands. These are the companies that believe in their products and commit to their customers. They may be hard to find, but I'm happy to report that they do exist.

BEYOND SELLING—HOW ADVERTISING IS AFFECTING HOW YOU THINK

What's less obvious about advertising but important not to overlook is that it doesn't just sell us things, it also sells us its own moral code. It has a significant amount of power to shape our beliefs by showing us what's acceptable and what's not. Currently, it mostly shows us a strange, fun-house mirror version of our world, where everyone has over-white teeth, thigh gaps, and immaculate houses, and people of color are tolerated so long as they are not "too black."

Shocked? Yes, me too. Yet that's the reality. A lot of progress toward equality has been made but, from my experience in ad land, there's still some way to go.

A couple of years ago I was writing a TV ad for a breakfast product and was specifically asked to show lots of different types of people enjoying it, so I wrote a gay couple into the script. The client feedback was that we *could* have two men in the four-second scene "so long as they didn't touch, flirt, or look at each other too long."

"So they want roommates," I said. "They can't be gay because?" I never got an answer to that question, and my colleagues couldn't understand why I was furious. "I'm gay and *I'm* not offended, so how can you be?" said my account manager. "Okay," I explained. "Imagine a young gay person overhearing this conversation, that a huge global company won't have gay people in their ad because they're worried sales of their product will go down. What kind of message does that kid get? That they're not going to be accepted—that their mere existence can put people off their breakfast."

That ad was shelved, so the argument never escalated; but a year later, I managed to persuade the same client to cast an interracial family. However, when I chose the actors, the client came back saying that they would not accept my casting because my choices were "too black." Feeling there must be some misunderstanding, I asked if there was any other reason why they didn't like those actors. "No," came the reply. It was purely a matter of skin tone. I tried everything I could think of, including threatening to quit, to persuade my bosses to insist on the hiring, but I was told, "We can't afford to lose them as a client," and in the end, although my agency strongly voiced their objection, they gave in and the ad was recast with lighter-skinned people. It was this incident more than anything that spurred me to do something else with my life.

So now, how can we who are horrified by the idea of prejudice counter the messages we get from ads? The best defense I know against prejudice is empathy.

GENERATING EMPATHY

So much of the imagery we see, in ads and other areas of life, can divide us into "us" and "them," "the haves" and "the have-nots," and actively undermine our happiness by preventing us from connecting and empathizing with others. In order to counteract this, here's an exercise specifically to help you generate more empathy.

- Spend twenty minutes on the Humans of New York website (www.humansofnewyork.com) or reading human-interest stories in the newspaper. There are stories there from people of every background and walk of life. Some are funny and some are deeply moving.

- Pick a person you wouldn't normally meet. Look into their eyes.

- Now, take a deep breath, close your eyes, and try to imagine yourself in their skin, seeing the world as they do. Imagine going about your day as that person.

- Imagine meeting yourself as that person. How do you react? Do you ignore yourself, or do you engage? Can you find common ground?

I believe my experiences in advertising shine a light on why we need to question the messages that we see and I hope that through this questioning we can override the subconscious messaging from companies that may not share our values. Only this will leave us free to make our own choices.

SHOULD WE BAN ALL ADS?

Having read this far, you may be thinking, "If advertising is so bad, why not ban it?" If we could click our fingers and get rid of it all, should we? I might be tempted, but no.

At its heart, all advertising is a mass sharing of information, and it doesn't even have to be for commercial gain. It's often useful in telling us about things we might not otherwise have known about and services that are available to us. Plus, sometimes there are puppies involved!

However, I am one of the growing number of people who believe we should have a choice over whether we see ads in our daily life or not. As we found out in Chapter 1, ads do harm us by triggering materialism. We can choose to forgo certain TV channels and publications to avoid certain ads. However, without closing our eyes and bumping into things, it's impossible for us to avoid the posters and billboards plastered all over cities. Phasing out these street ads isn't as far-fetched as it sounds. In 2016, a group raised funds to replace all of the advertisements in one London underground station with pictures of cats. So for one glorious week, the residents of Clapham got tabbies instead of tablet ads.[7] And in São Paulo, Brazil, the city council has banned all outdoor advertising. Fifteen thousand billboards have been taken down, which has completely changed the identity of the city.

There are now channels, apps, and publications offering you the choice to pay if you don't want to see advertisements. This could be seen as a step forward, but there is the danger that it could force poorer people to watch ads while the rich can afford to avoid them. This idea was taken to its extreme in an episode of *Black Mirror* that showed a dark future where everyone lived in tiny rooms, their walls entirely made out of TV screens.[8] Ads blazed at them all day long, but if they wanted to close their eyes and shut it out, they had to pay. If they ran out of credit, they were forced to keep their eyes open and lap it up . . . shudder.

Like many things, the power of advertising can be harnessed for the dark side, the light, or the myriad of grays, beiges, and bubblegum pinks in between. I know there are people in ad land who want to have a positive impact on the world, but think that they can't afford to have a conscience. That doesn't have to be true. I've moved away from talking about the products that I don't feel are beneficial to humanity and chosen to put my effort into brands that I believe in. If advertising agencies started to seek out game-changing ethical businesses and spread the word about them, these companies might grow to disrupt more complacent and damaging big businesses.

Advertising people might feel that they're just cogs in the wheel, but cogs can spin in both directions. Maybe, if the advertising industry empowered itself to change, it could spin its cog the other way, and take the rest of commerce with it. So, if you're one of the millions of people who work in marketing, PR, or advertising, get in touch. There's a lot we can do.

4

Marketing

or

The Ten Tactics That
Make Us Spend

Advertisers like us to believe that we aren't influenced by their tricks. But we *are*, even if we're not aware of it. Rance Crain, once the editor of *Advertising Age*, explains, "Only 8 percent of an ad's message is received by the conscious mind. The rest is worked and reworked by the recesses of the brain."[1] We might not run straight out and buy the product, but it's clear that ads have an effect because the people who watch the most ads save less, spend more, and work more hours to pay for the things they feel they need to buy.[2]

To help you to practice mindful curation effectively, this chapter reveals the ten most effective tactics marketers use to put us under their spell, and the counter-curses we can employ to defend ourselves against them.

TACTIC 1: GET US YOUNG

We are conditioned from birth to recognize brands. Disney now hands out free onesies to get their logo in front of infants' eyes (even if those eyes can't focus yet), ensuring that they will be able to sell to these kids for years to come.[3] When I was a baby in 1983, just $100 million was spent on marketing to kids. Now it's more than $17 *billion*.[4] It's been shown that babies, at six months old, can recognize logos and mascots;[5] that at the age of three, they can recognize 100 brands; and that they will demand the brands they know as soon as they can talk.[6] My niece, at three years old, would joyfully quote a "mold and mildew spray" ad by heart. At the time, we thought this was hilarious but it does bring it home that kids are taking all this in, even if we think the TV is just on in the background.

Does this matter? I would argue it mainly depends on the content of the commercials. The average child sees around 40,000 commercials a year,[7] and young kids don't understand that commercials are trying to sell something, they just see them as another story.[8] For me, the negative and disturbing imagery that makes up roughly 13 percent of ads isn't the only negative thing about commercials. Almost every food ad that kids see is for unhealthful food; as a result, for every extra hour of television kids watch, they eat an additional 167 calories.[9]

Most crucially for our kids, ads are the top pushers of the materialism drug—the mechanism that makes us crave material objects at the same time as isolating us from each other. In 1978, researchers studied two groups of kids. One group watched a TV show that included toy commercials, and the other watched it without. Later, the kids who had watched the ads chose to play alone with the advertised toys instead of with their friends in the sandbox.[10] Today, TV isn't the only place selling to children; 87 percent of the most popular websites for kids include advertisements.[11]

Another popular tactic marketers use is called "cross promotion." This is where they take our kids' favorite characters and use them to sell unrelated products, usually fast food. Kids trust these familiar heroes who are so good and noble in stories. So of course, they would never suspect their favorite character was pushing food that was bad for them.

What to do?

Here are a few ways you can protect your kids from commercial overload.

- Campaign for a commercial-free childhood: www.commercialfreechildhood.org.

- Be aware that the American Academy of Pediatrics recommends no screen time at all until the age of two. And there is no evidence that TV and computer products designed for babies increase their ability to learn language.[12]

For older children:

- Skip ads on TV and get an ad-blocker on your family computer.

- Listen to music or audio books instead of commercial radio.

- Most important, teach children what ads do.
    - Watch some ads together and encourage them to question what they are seeing, especially if what's shown doesn't match your values.
    - Explain that ads are trying to sell something and don't always show the truth, but use exaggeration, cleverness, funny words, and celebrities to make kids like something.

- Explain that advertising makes them want new toys and not like the toys they already have as much. To counteract this, help your kids write fun ads for the toys they already have so that they appreciate them.

TACTIC 2: REAL FAKERY

Advertisers know that we're more likely to buy something if the ad feels "real." When I worked in advertising, we even used to cast real parents and their kids in our commercials so that we could leverage their genuine love and intimacy to sell stuff. Ick! But some of the information ads give is as false as the false eyelashes they peddle. In fact, in one Cover Girl mascara ad, they claim their product is so good "You may never go false again." But if you looked in the corner of the page, you'd see a tiny smudge of writing admitting that the model pictured is, in fact, wearing false lashes. This is just the tip of the iceberg when it comes to the deception in advertising.

In one of the ads I filmed, we had to use a kid's treat from a rival brand to get the "enjoyment shot" on the kids' faces as they chewed, as they had repeatedly spat out the actual treat in disgust. "Hopefully no one will ever find out we did that," said the account manager as we left the shoot. It's not only the food that can be fake. Showing "real people" reacting to a product makes the viewer feel that they can trust the brand more. However, people in ads are never "real people." They might not seem like actors, but:

1. They probably are actors—or want to be actors.

2. Even if they're not actors, they've chosen to appear in a commercial and they'll usually have been paid to do so.

3. Even if they have not been paid, they know they have a camera on them and are expected to be positive about the product.

4. If there's any danger of real people reacting the wrong way, the ad agency will film enough people to show some of them loving the product.

Many of the statistics in ads are also based on very small sample sizes or surveys skewed by the lure of a competition, misleading language, or tricky surveying. For example, Colgate ran a billboard campaign proudly stating, "80 percent of dentists recommend Colgate," which led people to assume that the other brands were inferior, with only 20 percent of dentists recommending them. In fact, when the dentists were asked which brands they liked, they could pick several, so other brands could have been equally or more popular.[13]

What to do?

There's only one solution to this issue: If in doubt (and we should *always* be in doubt when it comes to ads), trust no one and nothing. If this sounds depressing, fear not. There are plenty of excellent places to get information to help you make buying choices, including customer reviews, unbiased experts, consumer reports, and Chapter 11.

TACTIC 3: SOCIAL MANIPULATION

The holy grail of advertising is when an ad campaign manipulates the whole of society to create a new norm. For example, when men go out to buy engagement rings, they're often told the rule is that they have to spend between one and three months' salary. But where did this rule come from? I asked a few of my friends and family if they knew. "Tradition?" they answered vaguely.

In fact, it was a brutally clever advertising campaign by De Beers, the diamond brand. They ran ads saying, "How else can you make two months' salary last forever?" Not only did De Beers set this arbitrary price on love, they created the idea of diamond engagement rings in the first place. In the 1940s, only 10 percent of engagement rings had diamonds. Then De Beers ran their famous "A diamond is forever" campaign and by the 1990s, 80 percent of engagement rings were twinkly bits of carbon.[14] Nowadays, the rule that an engagement ring should be a diamond seems as old as marriage itself.

What to do?

The next time you find yourself buying something or spending a certain amount of money because "it's normal" or "everyone will expect it," remember that they only expect it because they've been told to expect it. There are no natural laws of humanity that say you have to buy anything. Think beyond the norms and put your money toward the things that will mean the most to you and serve your unique personality and situation the best.

TACTIC 4: COOL VS. CAREFUL

In 2012, a TV ad ran showing a series of small kids trying to resist Haribo sweets. They had been told that if they could resist the small squishy treat set before them for a few minutes, they could have another one. A funny montage ensued with kids picking up their sweets, putting them back down, sniffing them, and touching them with the tips of their tongues. One girl put her hand between herself and the sweet and exclaimed, "No, don't do it!" In the end, all the kids cracked and ended up eating the candy and an actress announced that Haribo was "just too good."[15] This ad, whether we realized it or not, was an instruction video on how we should behave around Haribo, i.e., give in to temptation.

Advertising has done a fantastic job of making it cool not to be careful. It celebrates impulsiveness and sneers at anything that speaks of self-control. This works for marketers, because the more we think things through, the less likely we are to buy something. What advertising wants from us is automatic responses.

What to do?

When it comes to decision-making, don't discount your first instincts, as they often have something valuable to say. But take the time to question that instinct when it comes to purchases. Of course, there are times to be completely in the moment. These can be the times that make life worth living. Just make sure there isn't a credit card in your hand.

TACTIC 5: CELEBRITY POWER

Celebrity culture and marketing are now so intertwined that sometimes you can't tell where a person ends and the brand begins. But taking a step back, it seems strange that you can take someone who is genuinely talented in one area and use them to sell something completely unrelated. Snoop Dog endorses Norton Antivirus, Justin Bieber endorses his own toothbrush, and Bob Dylan endorsed Victoria's Secret, but if I were looking for advice on cybersecurity, dental health, or how my breasts are best supported, these three celebs might be my very last port of call. There's not much logic to it, but marketers still do it, because it works. But why?

Research shows that we're much more likely to buy a product, and even spend up to 50 percent more on it, if we have "admiring envy" of a person who owns it.[16] The product could well be inferior in quality to its competitors, but because the celeb or vlogger gets us reacting emotionally, not rationally, we still want it. Admiring talented people is completely natural, but I would argue that we should not let that admiration extend to something they are trying to sell us. More often than not, they don't use or even like the products they endorse. David Beckham certainly didn't let his endorsement of Samsung get in between him and his iPhone.[17]

What to do?

The next time you see an ad featuring a celebrity you like, examine your feelings. I, for example, have a huge girl-crush on Jennifer Lawrence and it's easy for my positive feelings and her personality to transfer to the Dior bag in her hand. Suddenly it looks quite quirky, cute, and cool, just like her! If I want to know if I *actually* like the handbag, I need to do the following exercise.

FREE YOURSELF FROM CELEBRITY INFLUENCE

- Look at the celebrity in the ad and then think of another famous person you deeply dislike and imagine them in the advertisement instead.

- Picture it clearly and you should immediately feel differently about the product. The two celebs should cancel each other out in your mind, allowing you to decide whether you actually like the product for itself.

- Finally, it's worth remembering that if, for example, I did buy a Dior handbag, Jennifer Lawrence would sadly not be attached to it, *I'd* be attached to it, so it should reflect who *I* am, not be a second-hand reflection of her.

TACTIC 6: VIRAL ADS

When I worked in advertising, I dreamed of making a viral ad that people would actually *enjoy* watching. These are crafted not to look like ads at all. People send them to their friends to entertain them, meaning they can reach huge audiences and cause astronomical sales. In 2014, a video showing twenty strangers kissing for the first time was put up on YouTube. To date, this ad that doesn't look like an ad has attracted more than 1 billion views[18] and caused the sales of the clothing brand that made it to go up by 14,000 percent.[19]

When it comes to viral advertising, we may vaguely know we're being manipulated, but often we don't care because the humor or warm fuzzy feelings the video gives us seem worth it. So we share someone else's marketing message with our friends and family without stopping to consider what we're actually promoting.

What to do?

When you come across viral ads, enjoy them by all means, but don't confuse the sometimes powerful, moving messages in the videos with the actual values and actions of the company. If you see a viral video by a company that doesn't *act* in line with your values, try to resist sharing it, no matter how much you belly laughed or wept.

TACTIC 7: SEX APPEAL AND CREATING AN IDEAL

You can tell the ad team is out of ideas when they drape an almost-naked woman on the product. They know we're programmed to notice sexual cues, so sadly this lazy approach often works. The side effect is that women's bodies are turned into objects, which dehumanizes us, allowing society to feel that women are things to be owned, which can lead to violence against them. Often bodies in the ads are also completely manufactured. In some cases, pictures of four or five women might be pieced together to produce one "perfect" image. Why? Images of startlingly perfect faces and bodies are especially good at selling things. They captivate our attention because we are all very attuned to "health cues" in others—it's an instinct that has kept us safe down the years and encouraged us to breed with healthy people.

But this instinct is now being harnessed to sell us everything from sofas to soup.

This perfection process is used even on the extremely young. Before I was in advertising, I worked at a magazine for 7- to 11-year-old girls, and even children this age were airbrushed to perfection—to sell magazines. This action can have a terrible power. A study carried out three years after television was introduced to Fiji showed that cases of girls vomiting to lose weight went from 0 to 11.3 percent. And dieting, which was practically unheard of in Fijian culture in 1995, had rocketed to 69 percent of teenage girls.[20]

The people we are shown in ads are usually younger, whiter, taller, and thinner than average. Agencies hesitate to sign models older than eighteen because a model is "too old" at twenty-four. All of this comes together to make the rest of us feel old, fat, wrinkled, ugly, and insecure. And guess what insecurity does? It triggers our compulsive shopping.[21] We spend to fill the void because we'll never be as perfect as the ads say we should be.

What to do?

Counteracting body insecurity is all about building self-worth and healthy attitudes with regard to appearance. So:

- Every time you have a critical thought about your body, counteract it with a grateful thought about the amazing things it allows you to do. Revel in its ability to take you through life.

- Think of your body as something that relies on you completely to take care of it, just as a baby does. You don't judge a baby for its pudginess—you stroke it, give it unconditional love, encourage it to make the most of its talents, help it stay healthy. Do the same for your body. And the next time you see an ad that tells your subconscious you need something to feel okay about your body, your subconscious will answer for you, "We're fine, thanks."

- As well as helping your own self-esteem, if you are interested in joining the fight to help future generations, sign up at womennotobjects.com. This campaign uses four criteria to judge a commercial:

  o Is the woman being used as a prop—reduced to a thing?

  o Is she plastic—retouched beyond what's humanly possible?

  o Can we see only her body parts rather than her face?

  o How would you feel if she were your mother, daughter, sister, co-worker, or *you*?

If any of the above make you feel an ad has crossed a line, bring it to the attention of the #womennotobjects campaign. Brands will only change if we give them a reason to, so be vocal on social media when you don't like what they're doing.

TACTIC 8: FEAR TACTICS

If you google "fear of missing out [FOMO] in advertising," as I have, you'll find the top results are articles written to help marketers use FOMO to build their profits. They write that "users who experience FOMO can be encouraged to make purchases influenced by their fear. Because of this, it's an incredibly useful tool for marketers that shouldn't be overlooked."[22] "People want what they fear they can't have," delights another writer.[23] In fact, psychological studies have shown that we are twice as motivated to avoid a loss as we are to receive a gain, and around 40 percent of us admit that we get uneasy when we learn that some of our friends or peers are doing something that we are not.[24]

Marketers create FOMO by making what they're selling seem scarce or likely to be gone at any moment. "Limited edition," "limited time only," "flash sale," "ending soon," and one-off discounts and events are all part of this strategy, as is the use of an urgent voice. Urgent voices are usually associated with danger, so our primal brain thinks, "This might help me survive," and so we listen. One of my old clients was a sofa-maker so notorious for constantly screaming that their sale was ending that people would joke that if their sale ever *did* end, the world would too.

The crazy thing to me is that every time they said the sale was ending, people actually rushed to stores. So my client had constant sales, just so they could end them!

What to do?

Fear of missing out on a bargain can pressure us into making expensive mistakes. So, train your brain to be immune.

- The next time you see FOMO tactics, yawn, and say to yourself, "in another couple of months, they'll have another 'one-time' offer."

- Mindfully plan what you're going to buy and then do some research, using price-tracker tools, for the best times of year to get it.

- A lot of FOMO now comes from seeing other people on social media. So, unfollow (there are apps available to help with this) or mute people who tend to induce the most FOMO in you. Scrolling through idealized pictures of other's lives increases anxiety and decreases happiness. There will always be someone somewhere having a great time. We need to make peace with that and plan what *we're* going to do. Also, try to resist posting things that create FOMO in others. If we want to break this cycle, we should start with ourselves.

TACTIC 9: MAKING ADVERTISING
THAT ISN'T ADVERTISING

There's a secret war being waged—for our attention. With more people using ad-blockers and video on-demand services, advertisers have had to be more creative in what they do to get inside our heads. Here are some of their strategies.

Branded content

Comedy Central has gotten around the fact that only 20 percent of us pay attention to televised ads[25] by making short programs that are commercials in disguise. *Handy*, for example, is a series of five-minute films about a hand model. Each episode is sponsored by a different brand, such as Black & Decker and Joe's Crab Shack. They're funny. They're clever. They feel like a Comedy Central show. They do not mean you need a Black & Decker power drill.

Product placement

Companies will pay millions to get their products in TV shows and movies. BMW paid $3 million to be placed in the 1995 James Bond film *GoldenEye*, but made back $240 million in advance sales alone.[26] When done too blatantly, product placement might put us off, but often products are just there in the background, unnoticed by our conscious brain but lapped up by our subconscious. Then, one day we'll be shopping and feel drawn toward a particular brand, and may end up buying something inferior, or less appropriate for our needs, all because of a romcom we can't even remember.

The solution? Rational research. Question why you like the brands you do, look at their competitors, and seek independent advice on their quality, craftsmanship, and ability to serve your needs in the long term.

Sponsorship

The reason brands spend millions in sponsorship is so they can benefit from the positive feelings we have while watching those events. We unconsciously start to associate their logo with our joy, enthusiasm, and excitement.

The irony of fast-food brands sponsoring sporting events showcasing athletes who probably eat incredibly healthily never ceases to amuse me. All we can do in this case is be mindful of the sponsorship. When you are at an event, notice the brand names around you. If you don't like the idea of your subconscious remembering them in a positive light, rename them in your head, or come up with your own ad slogan to match how you think of them.

"Native advertising" and advertorials

These are advertisements disguised as news. For example, the *New York Times* ran an article all about energy, but it was sponsored by an energy company, so it was very difficult for it not to be biased.[27] Native advertising is particularly manipulative, because fewer than half of us can tell the difference between these articles and real ones.

Beware the advertorial. If you find yourself being convinced by a newspaper article that a product is just what you need right now, check to see if it says "advertorial" in the corner and then look for other sources of information on the product.

Using our friends to sell to us

Marketers know that we naturally trust our friends, so many have moved on to what's known as "social selling," making us advertise to each other. Marc Jacobs, for example, invited some of their trendy target audience to a pop-up shop and gave them free products in exchange for tweeting their hashtag.[28] These tweets were then seen by the patrons' friends, and Marc Jacobs managed to reach an audience they might not have been able to influence otherwise. When you see tweets or posts by friends talking about brands and products, just be aware that they may well have been given something, or are hoping to win something, and their endorsement isn't necessarily genuine. If a pal starts spamming regularly, the mute or unfollow button is just a short click away.

Conversely, unless you really believe in a product's value and would actually run up to a friend and tell them about it face-to-face, don't start talking about it in your feed because you're hoping to win a free prize. You then become part of the problem.

TACTIC 10: USING NEUROSCIENCE

Don't underestimate the lengths that an advertiser will go to get through to the parts of you that you didn't even know existed. Marketers long ago started examining the brain in order to figure out which ads were most likely to hit home. At the beginning of the twentieth century, a series of tests was done where people were very briefly shown magazine spreads and then asked to remember what they had seen. All sorts of data was collected that could be used by advertisers to make a bigger impact on us—for example, using black text on a white background to grab a man's attention or red text on a white background to appeal to women.[29]

Ad agencies now test their ads on people who are hooked up to brain monitors to evaluate their responses. Nielsen Media Research is one of the companies providing these tests. They explain, "By using the latest neuroscience technologies, we help brands understand consumers' unconscious responses."[30] Brainwaves, facial responses, and eye tracking are all examined to generate data on how well every second of an ad is being responded to. The ad will be tweaked and tweaked again until it creates the desired response in the subconscious mind. Ads are designed to be "sticky," so they pop back into our head when we're faced with a brand or we're in a particular situation.

Unless we're willing to isolate ourselves from modern life, we can't block out *all* the messages that are trying to skew our values and desires. However, we can counteract them with our own messaging.

MAKE YOUR OWN ADVERTISEMENTS

Make ads for things you've identified as bringing you the most fulfillment and positivity. (*There are exercises on how to identify these in Chapter 8.*) For example:

- Family time

- Hanging out with close friends

- Being in nature

- Pursuing a creative passion

The following would be some of my ads for these:

- "Your family! The only people who have to love you anyway."

- "Friends! Keeping you sane since 1982."

- "Nature! Scientifically proven to make you happier, healthier, and better at thinking with your . . . brain?"

- "Writing! The only known cure for Tara's Grumpy Cow Syndrome."

You can also surround yourself with imagery that you've really thought about and that represents your values. Many people do this automatically—when they put an image of a lover, best friend, or beloved cockapoo on their phone, they're reminding themselves of what's important.

THE INNER AD-BLOCKER

Advertising has become so much a part of our lives that we don't notice it, much less question it. I have come to believe that it is a type of hypnosis. It is designed to speak directly to our subconscious mind. That's because our conscious mind asks tricky questions such as "Can I afford it?" and "What's it made of?" Meanwhile, our subconscious has moved into the ad and is busy making out with the models.

If advertising is a form of hypnotism, might we be able to protect ourselves through counter-hypnosis? I spoke to two hypnotherapists to see if there was a way of creating an inner ad-blocker. And it seems there is!

AD-BLOCKING

Hypnotherapist Helen Craven, DCH, says that the best defense against ads is to regularly remind your subconscious that you are good enough as you are. This can be done by repeating a mantra such as "I have everything I need to be happy" before you run the gauntlet of advertising downtown. Craven warns that when we're on automatic pilot, our minds are in the "alpha state," which leaves us susceptible to subliminal messaging. To counter this, she suggests being mindful and present when we're in a situation with lots of advertising. This brings in our "beta state," which is more discerning about what affects us. Here are some ways of doing it.

When walking around town

Stay mindful through a simple walking meditation. Concentrate on your footfalls and the breath in your body. If you do notice an ad, let yourself notice it fully and think, "I have all I need already, thank you."

When reading a newspaper or magazine

When faced with advertising you can't avoid, hypnotherapist Chloë Brotheridge, author of *The Anxiety Solution*, suggests using your imagination to make the ad seem silly or ridiculous. "Give the model a sad clown's face or the head of Donald Duck," she suggests. "This can help you to take the ad less seriously."

When watching TV

Both Craven and Brotheridge warn that when watching TV we are particularly susceptible as our conscious mind is muted. Fight back by getting into the habit of muting the commercials instead. Use the five minutes to do something productive where you can't see the TV—tidy up, arrange to meet a friend, or floss!

SEPARATE LIFESTYLE AND PRODUCT

Here's another way to create an inner ad-blocker.

- If you find yourself tempted by a product in an ad, squint your eyes and just focus on the product. Let the lifestyle and messaging fade away.

- Now imagine having the product in your life. It's unlikely to appear the way it does in the ad. For example, if I owned a particular handbag, I'd probably not be clutching it while lying across a chaise longue as a scantily clad Latin gentleman kissed my neck, but instead plonking it down on the kitchen counter along with the cat food. Does the product you're craving still have the same allure in your real surroundings? If it doesn't pass this test, it's not the product for you.

Through using our inner ad-blocker, we should be freer to decide which products are really right for us and which are all sizzle, no steak. Now on to a particularly sizzle-prone category of products: clothing.

5

Faster and Faster Fashion

or
Getting Off the Trend Treadmill

*"Fashion—a field of ugliness so absolutely unbearable
that we have to alter it every six months."*
—OSCAR WILDE

We used to have two fashion seasons a year, but now, thanks
to fast fashion, we are offered new styles on a weekly basis
and it's considered newsworthy when a celebrity is seen
wearing the same dress twice. The implication is that if you
can afford it, you should constantly be wearing something
new. This has had a huge impact on our buying habits. In
1930, the average woman owned nine outfits, but now she
buys sixty-seven items of clothing every year.[1] Interestingly,
millennial men are now out-spending women on clothes for
the first time.[2]

This chapter asks how trends come about and why we are drawn to follow them. Are we any happier as a result of all this extra clothing? And how can we build a BuyMeOnce wardrobe based on our own style?

TRENDS

"Trendy is the last stage before tacky."
—KARL LAGERFELD

I was eighteen and just beginning to buy my own shoes when suddenly the style changed from round-toed to sharp points. I remember looking at a fashion billboard, turning to my friend and saying, "Even the models look weird in these." But just a few months later, I was replacing my round-toed pumps with a pair of pointy Carvelas, and the first time I put them on I felt sophisticated, fashionable, and not at all weird . . . unless you counted the pinched toes.

This is how trends work. If enough fashion or interior designers get behind a trend, you start looking at what you have and feeling that it's not quite up to snuff. The more "fashionable" and "on trend" a product style is on release, the shorter its life cycle tends to be. The industries can be assured that their products will look passé in a few years' time, forcing us to buy again.[3] And so, the great designer disco-ball can keep turning. As professional trend-tracker Martin Raymond admits, "Trends are profits waiting to happen." No wonder designers, decorators, retailers, vloggers, stylists, PR spinners, and advertising gurus are all fighting for the power to set trends. But who really holds the power? Anyone who's seen my favorite TV series, *Game of Thrones*, will know the truth about power—that it "resides with whoever we believe it resides with." That being the case, we can start to empower ourselves and see that there is no reason why it can't reside within ourselves.

And we, the small folk, need to take back the power, because trends are not our friends. Trends are like self-obsessed frenemies—they seem super-fun at first, but after a while you realize everything is done on *their* terms and they don't care if they make you uncomfortable or embarrass you at parties. They don't care if zigzag curtains give you a headache, skinny jeans make you look like a turkey in tights, or a buzz cut makes your head look too small for your body. In the end, you realize the only reason they're friends with you is because you massage their needy little egos. No one needs friends like these.

Why do we follow trends then? I believe there are three main reasons. First, when we were ancient humans crawling around the forest trying to figure out what was poisonous, copying successful people was a good survival tactic. But now companies are taking advantage of this instinct to sell us jeggings. The second reason is that being able to spot trends and follow the unwritten rules "correctly" is intimately linked with our damaging obsession with status. It's one of the many ways we've found to rank ourselves against each other, sort the in-crowd from the outcasts. It's not "cool" if *anyone* can do it. For the "cool" to keep ahead of the game, the rules have to change faster. That's how we ended up with the dizzying fast-fashion turnover we have now. The third driver of trends is boredom. It's probably not surprising that "Won't I get bored?" is one of the most common questions I'm asked about living a life less throwaway. The idea of committing to wearing the same things or having the same decor for a significant period of time fills people with anxiety.

It seems that modern humans are so afraid of being bored that when given a choice between sitting quietly in a room with their own thoughts or electrocuting themselves, most people will choose to give themselves painful electric shocks.[4] Changes in fashion trends rely on boredom. Mary Quant writes, "All a designer can do is to anticipate a mood before people realize that they are bored with what they have already got. It is simply a question of who gets bored first. Fortunately, I am apt to get bored pretty quickly."[5] We all get bored, and I'd argue that we need to get bored—it's part of human nature and it drives us toward playfulness, creativity, and invention. It needn't drive us to replace our clothes or household products. It's said that variety is the spice of life, but look at all the other spices available to us—what we do, where we go, who we meet, what we create, what we learn, and what we contribute to the world. There are an amazing number of new experiences out there that don't include a new top or snazzier throw cushions. It's time to think bigger.

When you feel bored, engage your curiosity. Complete the sentence "I've always wondered about. . . ." If you find yourself wondering, even very slightly, about any subject, place, experience, or person, follow that thought to see where it leads. You may uncover an unexpected passion—and wouldn't that be more interesting than a new type of T-shirt?

FAST FASHION

My laptop is showing me a young woman with wide blue eyes and tumbles of glossy hair. She talks confidingly into the camera as though I'm a pal she's known since we ate bugs together at nursery school. At this moment, Zoella is one of the most popular vloggers in the world, making more than $70,000 a month.[6] The video I'm watching is a Primark "haul" video.[7] She hefts a bag as big as herself onto her bed and proceeds to go through the stash. First up is a maxi shirt dress, staggeringly cheap at $18. Then a pair of shiny rose-gold Converse lookalikes. She explains cheerfully, "I thought they'd be really nice to throw on, and because they were only $11, I feel that it doesn't matter if these get ruined." She's fully aware that she's buying clothing and shoes that aren't meant to last, but in her mind their cheap price means this is fine. In the end, the haul is about forty items, ranging between $2 to $18 each. This is fast fashion at its most seductive. And it's not just vloggers who go binge shopping. On average, we buy 60 percent more than we did fifteen years ago and we keep our clothes for half as long.[8] This change may have been cheap for us, but it's costing other people dearly.

In 2015, a Norwegian documentary showed what happened when three fashion-mad teenagers went to Cambodia to experience the reality behind the fast-fashion clothing they loved.[9] The three young fashionistas stayed with a 25-year-old garment worker named Sokty. "My bathroom is bigger than her whole house," said the delicately blonde Anniken, her eyes wide in horror. Sokty works seven days a week, twelve hours a day. On Sundays, she "only has to work eight hours." When she was little, she dreamed of becoming a doctor, but now she sews jackets that cost the same amount that she makes in a year.

Before the Norwegians went to Cambodia, their attitude toward the garment workers could be summed up as "at least they have a job and things are different over there— they're used to hard work." Then they met a woman whose mother had died of starvation and another who had sewn the same seam on the same sweater twelve hours a day for fourteen years. Anniken had an abrupt change of heart. "No one should have to spend their day sewing until they collapse from dehydration and exhaustion. We are rich because they are poor—we can buy a T-shirt for $8, but someone had to starve so that we could buy it that cheaply."

Bangladesh has the second-largest garment industry in the world. On April 23, 2013, cracks appeared in the side of a Bengali clothing factory. The building was evacuated, but despite their protests, the garment workers were forced back to work the next morning, being told that they would lose a whole month's pay if they refused to reenter the building. At 8:57 a.m., with everyone inside, the building collapsed;

1,129 people were killed and more than 2,500 were injured. The Rana Plaza tragedy captured the world's attention for a few days, but the misery of what many call "modern-day slave labor" has continued, with those who protest their near-starvation wages and dangerous conditions simply being fired, beaten, or arrested.

What's the answer?

It's hard to hold this kind of story in mind when you're browsing for something pretty to wear on vacation. We don't think of sad, undernourished people at rows of sewing machines; we see the cheap prices, latest styles, and pretty embroidery. That's why I think, first, it's important to decide which brands share our values before we even start shopping. Finding brands that don't exploit their workers is incredibly easy—a quick search for "ethical clothing brands" will bring up a list. For those of us who've become used to the super-cheap pricing of big-box stores, the expense may feel jarring, but with these ethical and fair-trade brands we can be sure that, right down the line, people are being treated well and are getting what we would consider a fair living wage.

Second, consider organic clothing. The chemicals and pesticides used in the fashion industry may be one of the least-talked-about issues, but in the villages and cities where the cotton crops are grown and the clothes are treated and dyed, the chemicals get into the local drinking water in huge volumes. You'll even see bright-blue dogs wandering around. In some villages in India, the number of children born with birth defects, mystery illnesses, and cancers has skyrocketed. If we all bought organic clothes, not only would it be better for our own skin, but it would help save the health of unborn children half a world away.

Third, always think about the longevity of the garment. Buying long-lasting clothes is one of the easiest and, frankly, most pleasurable things we can do for the environment. If we can each increase our wardrobe's lifespan by just one to two years, it would reduce the fashion industry's CO_2 emissions over that year by 24 percent[10] and save billions of gallons of our increasingly precious water supply.

But longevity isn't just about sturdy fabric, it's also about choosing styles you're happy to wear for the long term and this means stepping off the trend treadmill.

FIND YOUR OWN STYLE AND BUILD A BUYMEONCE WARDROBE

The constant churn of trends often lures us into buying things that aren't right for our bodies or style. In this way, we are all fashion victims, and this section offers victim support and practical steps to make fashion work for you. But how to deal with the trend treadmill? Do we plonk our butts on the floor, refuse to play anymore, and wear onesies for the rest of our lives? Ironically, the clue to fashion salvation been given to us by one of the world's biggest fashion houses. It was Yves Saint-Laurent who famously stated, "Fashions fade, style is eternal."

For me this means finding your "soul style," the look you're happy to commit to. As in marriage, you want your "chosen one" to make you feel comfortable, bring out all your best qualities, and give you a glow even on a tough day. To begin, and this may pinch a little, unsubscribe from all fashion magazines, style bloggers, newsletters, and mailing lists. Any style inspiration or brand information you take in should come to you on your own terms, at least while you're still exploring your look. Finding your "soul style" isn't a quick process, but what it lacks in swiftness, it makes up for in fun. So let's get to it!

YOUR FASHION IDENTITY, OR WHY EVERYONE SHOULD DRESS LIKE MY FRIEND BEN

If clothes were solely a way of stopping our naughty bits from getting frostbite, we'd probably all just wear the same thing—(I vote pajamas!). But clothing has taken on layers of meaning and symbolism that have become so complex that even an extra inch of fabric at the ankle or wrist can make the difference between someone looking well-dressed or silly, or maybe unhinged and potentially dangerous. If you don't believe me, imagine sitting on the subway and seeing a middle-aged man in a suit with trousers that end halfway down his calf. You would wonder, Did he pick up the wrong trousers? Is he trying to make a fashion statement? Is he unhinged? Or going to a costume party? You would probably watch his behavior for clues. He's broken a norm of society, so what else might he do?

When it comes to choosing my own style, I'm happy to dress as "normally" as necessary to assure the people around me I'm not potentially dangerous. Beyond that, I mindfully curate my own style and wear whatever I want, but whenever I feel lost in my own fashion conviction I think of my friend Ben.

Thirty years old, tall, dark, and slim as a beanpole, on an average day Ben Shires might be seen wearing a tailored tweed jacket, waistcoat, vintage watch, tie-pin, and horn-rimmed glasses. The perfectly waxed hair completes a look that I can only describe as "Buddy Holly goes to Downton Abbey." Early on, he'd had an epiphany that he had very individual passions and interests (collecting stamps, old post-cards, and fossils) but he wasn't reflecting that in his dress. There was pressure to fit in with his friends, who were mainly wearing typical teenage tracksuits, but thankfully Ben was given brilliant advice that has stuck with him: "As soon as you change for someone else's reason, you stop being your-self." So now he wears only what *he* finds interesting and fun, which has led to a wonderfully original personal look.

Ben explains that following fashion means you end up embarrassed by what you wore ten years ago, even five years ago, and it's because fashion tells us to be embarrassed. He goes on to say, "I'm so outside the main fashion trend, there's no need to change. If you follow trends, you lose sight of what looks good on you, because you're trying to fit in with the fad, and that fad isn't right for everyone. If you develop your own style, you can't be dictated to by fashion. As long as I stay in shape, I'll be able to wear these clothes for the rest of my life."

I asked Ben, "If I snapped my fingers and everyone on the whole planet disappeared, do you think you'd still dress the same?" "Yeah," he laughed. "I dress like this even when there's no one to look at me, and I do put in the same amount of effort, because I think it's not just about the clothes, it's the mentality. It's the philosophy of how you treat yourself."

When I asked Ben if he thought fashion could communicate who you truly are, we reached an interesting contradiction. He believes that the way he dresses reflects who he is and helps him to be more himself. However, he also said, "There are lots of misconceptions about what clothes mean. For example, some people think that because I pay attention to the way I dress, I'm not masculine and therefore wouldn't like soccer, which is funny, because I host a soccer TV show!"

This got me thinking about how much clothing can tell people about us and I concluded that when it comes to our passions and the *really* important things about our humanity, clothing can leave us in the dark. It can't tell us, for example, who would be a faithful friend or a great parent or who would make us laugh until we cry. However, beyond this limitation there are two useful powers it does possess. It indicates how we want the world to respond to us and the role we want to play in it. So when I say that we should all dress like my friend Ben, I don't mean "never without a waistcoat." Ben has managed to find a look that completely resonates with his identity and the roles he plays in his life. These next two exercises should help you do the same.

FINDING YOUR FASHION IDENTITY

This exercise is designed to ensure the clothes you buy are in line with your character and values. Below is a chart of personality traits. In a range of 1 to 5, write down where you want to be. For example, if you'd like to be seen as very approachable, check 1; a bit approachable, check 2. If you're not bothered either way, check 3. If you'd like to be seen as a bit aloof, check 4, and very aloof, check 5. (That's where you want to be, not necessarily the way you think people see you now.)

PERSONALITY TRAITS	1	2	3	4	5
approachable–aloof					
extroverted–introverted					
country–city					
adventurous–safe					
countercultural–conservative					
lighthearted–serious					
buzzy–calm					
feminine–masculine					
modern–traditional					
hi-tech–natural					
extravagant–thrifty					
tough–delicate					
fierce–sweet					
ambitious–laid-back					
controlled–relaxed					
mature–youthful					
sexual–platonic					
individualistic–anonymous					

Now, ignore all the ones where you answered 3, which means you're somewhere in the middle, and see what you get. To give an example, my results were:

> very approachable
> bit introverted
> very feminine
> bit traditional
> bit tough
> bit ambitious
> bit relaxed
> bit sexual

Finally, go through your closet and see if you feel your clothes are living up to the image that you want to portray. Not every piece will get the message across, but you can aim for your wardrobe, when taken as a whole, to represent you, or boost you in certain situations. For example, I feel I'm missing some natural toughness, so I might consider adding a leather jacket or sharp blazer.

DRESSING UP FOR THE ROLES YOU PLAY

One of my favorite authors, Caitlin Moran, wrote in her book *How to Be a Woman*, "When a woman says, 'I have nothing to wear,' what she really means is, 'there's nothing here for who I'm supposed to be today.'"[11] If you often go to your closet and find you have "nothing to wear," it may be that you haven't thought much about the roles you play in your life and the "costumes" you need to play them. So, make a list of your roles in your everyday life, from the most common roles to the rarest. If appropriate, add in how you'd like to be seen while playing those roles. For example, these are a few of mine:

continued

> mad author writing alone in a shed (not seen at all)
> CEO of a start-up (bright and competent)
> woman out with friends (comfortable and nice)
> wife out on date-night (hot)
> speaker at events (inspiring and memorable)
>
> Now, go through your wardrobe. Do you have something to wear for each of your individual roles? Do your clothes reflect how often you are called on to play those roles? If there are one or two outfits that can cover you for multiple roles, so much the better.

The second power I believe fashion has is to affect and enhance how we feel when wearing the clothes. Because of the powerful symbolism and physical presence that clothing has, it can become like a magic charm or mantra, helping us to embody the person we wish to be.

In her 2014 book *Mind What You Wear*, professor Karen Pine describes a series of experiments where she found that when she put her students into Superman shirts, they actually did better on exams; and students in white coats showed an increase in mental agility.[12] She goes on to lay out some of the ways our clothing affects us, including:

A statement piece that marks us as an individual will make us feel special.

Colors found in nature, such as sky blue and sunny yellow, can give us a mental boost of energy.

Loose, comfortable clothing can make us feel adventurous. Natural fabrics nurture us more than synthetics.

Playful patterns can bring out a playfulness in our mood.[13]

All of this should be kept in mind as we go from look-ing at fashion identity to looking at the pure aesthetic side of clothes shopping. Spending time to find what suits your body shape and coloring may seem like an effort but you only have to do it once, and it will empower you to let trends and fads pass you by.

SHAPE UP

The power of shape came home to me in a big way when I went wedding-dress shopping. One dress would make me look like an awkward, wobbly frump; the next, elegant, poised, and frankly better than I thought I ever could look in a dress.

In the past, we took the fabric we liked to a dressmaker, who would help us make the most of our body shape. But we usually don't do this today, and many of us haven't nailed down the shapes that suit us. If you haven't, take the time to do so now.

- Go to the biggest shop you can find. Before you go in, know that you're *not* there to buy anything.

- Try on as wide a range of shapes as possible, ideally in plain colors to prevent the patterns from distracting you.

- Now, using the following tables, mark each shape out of 5. (I've left room for you to add extra shapes you may find.)

continued

NECKLINES AND COLLARS	SCORE OUT OF 5
classic collar (button-down)	
club collar	
cutaway collar	
dog-eared blouse	
halter	
mandarin collar	
Peter Pan–collared blouse	
round high	
round low	
shawl-collared blouse	
sleeveless	
spread collar	
square neck	
straight high	
straight low	
sweetheart	
turtleneck	
V-neck high	
V-neck low	

SLEEVE LENGTH AND SHAPE	SCORE OUT OF 5
capped	
flared	
long	

loose	
short	
spaghetti	
three-quarter	
tight	
vest	

WAISTLINES	SCORE OUT OF 5
Empire	
high waist	
low waist	
mid-waist	

DRESS SHAPES	SCORE OUT OF 5
cinched waist	
flowing and flaring	
loose hanging	
skimming the waist	
tailored and structured	
tight	

continued

JACKETS AND COATS	SCORE OUT OF 5
cape	
car	
double-breasted	
drape jacket	
duffle	
long jacket/blazer	
mid-jacket/blazer	
motorcycle jacket	
pea	
princess	
quilted parka	
reefer	
short jacket/blazer	
single-breasted	
slim-shouldered	
tailored	
trench	
wide-shouldered	

SKIRT SHAPES	SCORE OUT OF 5
A-line	
ankle	
asymmetrical	
draped/wrap	

flared	
knee-length	
maxi	
mermaid	
mid-calf	
mini	
pleated	
tulip/bubble	

JEANS/TROUSER SHAPES	SCORE OUT OF 5
boot cut	
flared	
high waist	
hipster	
skinny	
standard waist	
straight cut	

Look back on your highest-scoring shapes, and use them to inform your purchases in the future. You may find you look great in many shapes, but make a note of the ones that particularly pop. It really saves shopping time if you can say, "I'm looking for a flare-skirted knee-length dress with a V- or sweetheart neckline."

FIND YOUR TRUE COLORS

*"The best color in the world is the one
that looks good on you."*
— COCO CHANEL

You can still pay to have your colors done, as many did in the 1980s, but you can also get a good idea of your colors on your own.

While you're in that huge shop, pick garments in as many different shades as you can. Hold them up just below your face in good lighting and rate the effect the color has. The right colors will make your complexion glow and your eyes pop. They'll draw the eye to *you* rather than the color itself.

If you're shopped out, you can do this at home. In natural light against a white background, take a good, clear close-up picture of your naked face with your hair down. Upload it to your computer and place multiple images of it next to different colors. Make a note of the colors that draw the eye to that particular face.

BUILDING A CAPSULE WARDROBE

"Buy less, choose well."
—VIVIENNE WESTWOOD

Now that you've had a chance to nail down both your fashion identity and the looks that suit you, you should be in good shape for putting together a "capsule wardrobe." A capsule wardrobe is what you would pack on a "half-work, half-pleasure" trip for two weeks to a place with variable weather where you can't do much laundry.

When I talked to Ben about his opinion on where most people go wrong when clothes shopping he said, "I think many people buy things only for 'this moment' or 'that event,' so they end up with a wardrobe stuffed with lots of stuff they don't care about. Building a capsule wardrobe allows you to take a step back and look at the whole picture and how it all works together. It need not be anonymous and utilitarian, as some pictures suggest. The curated capsule wardrobe should be as individual as you are and give you a burst of pleasure and well-being every time you open your closet door. I like to think of it as a pill that can cure us of materialism, nothing-to-wear-syndrome, and excess baggage fees at the same time.

THE MINDFULLY CURATED CAPSULE

The packing test

- Get out a suitcase (only one) and start packing.

- As you pack, think about your fashion identity and role findings from the previous exercises. Ask, "Does this piece reflect who I am and how I want the world to see me?"

- Choose only your A-list pieces (the ones you'd reach for first) and prioritize those that are versatile.

- Think about which clothes layer well to cope with the different seasons.

This suitcase is the beginning of your capsule wardrobe.

Look at what's left in your closet and drawers. Ask yourself if it deserves to remain. In the same way that we should never buy something mindlessly, we should never let something go mindlessly. It's worth questioning exactly why you let things go, so you can turn it into a pledge not to buy anything that might have similar problems in the future. For example, "This type of material is itchy or shows sweat marks" or "I can't cycle in it."

continued

If you want to keep reducing the amount of clothes after the initial cull but you genuinely use everything you have left, simply wear those clothes out and don't replace them until you get down to a more manageable number.

Buying in the future—your style cheat sheet

You may need to add to your capsule to complete it, so here's how to make sure everything you buy will be mindfully curated.

First, look at the clothes you have in your capsule and pick a couple of "hero pieces"—items that make you feel especially confident and attractive when you wear them.

Write them down and note what is it about them that you like. If it is the color, then in the future find other pieces that are that color or go with that color. If it is the shape, do the same.

Next, taking the knowledge that you have gained in the last few chapters, browse Google images using generic keywords such as *dresses* or *trousers*. Collect fifty images of clothes that you can imagine wearing every day and on special occasions. Now, use the images to answer the following five questions to create your "style cheat sheet."

1. Which colors come up most? Do these reflect your findings from the previous exercise? These are your core colors.

2. Which neutral colors—e.g., black, white, browns, and denim—work with several of your core colors?

3. Which accent colors (bright colors used sparingly) are you drawn to?

4. Which patterns or prints are you drawn to? What mood do the clothes reflect, e.g., smart, casual, flirty, light, or flamboyant?

5. Is any era coming to the fore? Do you recognize any cultural influences? Boho, hipster, rock, punk, preppy, pop culture, classic, modern?

Keep this cheat sheet on your phone or in a notebook and don't go shopping without it.

Building a shoe capsule

First, gather all of your shoes together—even the ones at the front door, in storage, under the bed, and unaccountably in the cat basket—and pick out your favorite pair for each of the following occasions:

a beach vacation
a winter vacation
casual-wear winter
casual-wear summer
formal-wear winter
formal-wear summer
work-wear winter
work-wear summer
exercising
relaxing at home

This is your core group, though you may need to add a specific pair or two, e.g., hiking boots. Each pair that you add to your core collection needs to bring something unique. Think first of the role it has to perform and the style that will give you the most versatility and flexibility and then ensure the quality of the shoe is as high as it can be. *(For advice on shoe quality, see Chapter 11.)*

continued

Now look at the extra shoes in your collection. Let them go if you haven't worn them in a year, find them uncomfortable, or you have similar shoes you prefer. Repair any damaged favorites.

Finally, put your shoe capsule collection back in your closet and admire!

Accessories

A specially chosen accessory can be a way to convey your signature style, a unique calling card by which people recognize you. I always wear my button-shaped pendant necklace and I have a friend who always wears a felt hat. These touches can also have the benefit of making you feel "put together." They're a signal that you've thought about your appearance and have made a polite and respectful effort.

If you want your other, more practical accessories to last as long as possible, it's worth going for classics. A capsule collection could include:

- Diamond stud earrings that will never go out of style and are as hard as, well, diamonds. You'll also have something to trade in an apocalypse.

- A cozy knitted cashmere hat or a Russian trapper hat to keep your ears warm.

- A classic cotton hat will keep heatstroke away. There are some on the market with a lifetime guarantee.

- A Turkish peshtemal, or "Turkish towel," that can be used as a scarf, wrap, blanket, bag, sarong, or towel and is perfect for both winter and summer holidays.

- A black leather belt is the most versatile. There are plenty of excellent leather brands offering long warranties.

- A durable travel umbrella with a lifetime warrantee.

- A dark-colored bag that will look better with age, can fit everything you need to carry daily, but isn't too heavy to carry for a couple of hours. *(For details on bag quality, see Chapter 11.)*

Above all, when it comes to your capsule, remember that fashion journalist G. Bruce Boyer states, "Real style is never right or wrong. It's a matter of being yourself on purpose."

THE "WORK UNIFORM"

Creative manager Matilda Kahl has worn the same outfit to work every day for four years. Not only has it saved her countless hours and dollars, it's also freed up brain space for her to be creative and released her from the pressure and stress of dressing to impress every morning. It's a strategy employed by some of the world's greatest thinkers to allow them to focus on what's important. Steve Jobs famously bought 100 Issey Miyake black turtlenecks, enough to last him a lifetime, and Mark Zuckerberg's gray T-shirt and hoodie combo has become iconic. But there's no need for a work uniform to be boring. The head of Pixar wears a raucously loud Hawaiian shirt every day.

How do you choose a work uniform?

There are several factors to take into consideration, including:

- The most formal and casual occasions that you will come across at work.

- The practicalities of your job. What will your body have to do physically? Do you have to stay on your feet for long hours? Might you get hot and sweaty at any point? Do you often go straight from work to social functions?

- The impression you want to give to your co-workers.

Start exploring and if you find a likely candidate, buy one set and wear it several times before committing to buying several. Color can be a way of bringing in variety if you crave it. When you're sure of the style you want, buy the highest-quality items you can afford. How do you spot that quality? See Chapter 11.

Finally, a note on compliments

We often compliment each other on our clothing—it's much easier than commenting on someone's character. But recently, I've realized that the friends I'm closest to now are the people I've spontaneously complimented on their nature. The first time I met one of my closest friends, I remember blurting out, "It must be awesome being friends with you— you'd never need a TV!"

Showing someone that you appreciate something about their nature is so much more fulfilling for you *and* for them than a comment on their possessions. So, the next time you find yourself about to compliment someone on their outfit, switch it up to compliment them on one of their character traits instead and see what happens.

6

Born to Shop

or

How Our Monkey Brain Influences What We Buy

The preteen tote bag had it right all along. We *are* "born to shop." As if we didn't have enough to contend with, with planned obsolescence and advertising, our very nature is stacked against us. But in this chapter I'll be showing you how we can counter our inner consumer, find value in who we are rather than what we own, and why this is crucial to our happiness.

OUR BUYER BRAIN:
TURNING LUXURIES INTO NECESSITIES

When a human is born, all it really needs to be happy is air, water, food, a reasonably comfortable environment, and positive connections with other humans. If a baby born today were sent back in time to live with a cave family, they could live as happy and fulfilled a life as they might today. Yet our modern culture, together with our human brain quirks, persuades us we need an excessive number of products in order to be happy.

There are two ways our brain contributes to our shopping habits. The first is that it becomes highly engaged by anything new. Thousands of years ago, when our ancestors were evolving, noticing new things helped them survive. It might be something dangerous—or a new food source. The second way our brain affects our purchasing is that once we're used to something, our gray matter tends to ignore it to save on processing power. So older objects stop exciting us and we want something new.

In ancient times, not using up brain power by actively noticing every familiar rock or mammoth would have been very useful. It meant there was extra brain space left over for hunting and keeping babies alive. Nowadays it means that we get excited by new trends or purchases and yet start taking them for granted extremely quickly. The exception to this is products that give us ongoing good and varied *experiences*—for example, a guitar, an heirloom cooking pot, or a car that's a joy to drive.

In the 1930s, Christine Frederick, of Chapter 2 fame, encouraged manufacturers to turn luxuries into necessities, and our brain's natural tendencies helped that process along. It took fifty years (between 1900 and 1950) for the cooking stove to go from being a luxury (with only 10 percent of the population having one) to a necessity (80 percent). In comparison, microwaves took just ten years to do the same.[1] Unless we're careful, we may have mass rollouts of products that, within a year, feel as much a necessity as a refrigerator feels today. This hedonic treadmill is speeding up, it seems, but there is a way to turn the treadmill back the way it came.

TURNING NECESSITIES INTO LUXURIES

This week, when you use your everyday items, take a minute with each one, close your eyes and imagine life without it. How would you get by without:

> your phone
> your computer
> your fridge
> your TV
> your car
> your stove
> your toaster/kettle/coffee maker
> your shower

I added "shower" to the list because one morning as I stood under the spray, I imagined the water drying up and the shower disappearing. I imagined having to pump water and boil it to wash myself. Suddenly, the warmth on my skin felt like a heavenly indulgence, and I left the shower full of gratitude.

BUYING FOR STATUS

A couple of years ago, I had a strange experience when I ran out of moisturizer while visiting my parents in Hong Kong. The drug store, like most around the world, had whole shelves of creams and potions, but as I looked along the rows, it was hard to find a moisturizer that *didn't* have some kind of skin-whitening properties. It seemed that Chinese women were obsessed with looking as pale as possible. This used to be the case in Britain, too. Queen Elizabeth I famously painted herself with lead paste to obtain a bone-white look (and poisoned herself in the process). Pale skin showed the world that you were a woman of delicacy and leisure who didn't have to go outside and work in the fields. In other words, it showed that you were too posh to plow.

This changed in the 1920s, when the poor worked indoors in factories and the rich went abroad for sunny vacations. Apparently, Coco Chanel got sunburned on the way to Cannes and started the tanning trend, which is now a massive industry in the West, while in China, women spend two billion dollars a year making themselves paler, as mentioned.[2] It all comes down to showing others our status. Obsession with status isn't a modern hang-up. When we first evolved as humans, we lived in small family tribes and it was important for us to know the strengths of each member of the group and who was mating with whom. Status has always been linked to strength, popularity, and intellect because these traits helped us find successful mates and survive beyond ourselves.

A weak infant might be ignored and the resources given to another child that had a higher likelihood of surviving. To be unpopular could mean death, to be ousted from the tribe, to lose access to help, care, and food. It's no wonder then that social status is one of the biggest drivers when it comes to our behavior. It's the reason we get so upset if someone is rude to us, even though they haven't hurt us physically. It questions our status and this brings up an ancient primal fear: Losing our status puts us in mortal danger.

This knowledge (whether it is understood fully or not) is used to sell us things. If you go online and look at the advertisements for the most expensive brands being sold right now, you'll see that many of the models will be looking straight into the camera in a disdainful, superior way, or even as if they want to murder you. If you came across this person in real life and they continued to look at you like that, you'd probably think, "Damn, they're rude." And they are. The model's expression is designed to make you question your status and to see them as superior so subconsciously you want what they have. Sold! We share our status obsession with many animals, including our closest cousins. In one of the more bizarre experiments I've come across, monkeys would give up some of their ration of fruit juice to be able to look at pictures of high-status monkeys in their group, but would prefer to look at a blank gray square than look at a picture of a lower-ranked monkey.[3]

Humans are the same with our celebrity culture; we gorge ourselves on media about people who don't know we exist and wouldn't care about us even if they did, but are still high status in our eyes. So the gossip magazines have evolution to thank for their sales. Our status-buying is also closely linked to our intense drive, especially as young adults, to be seen as good sexual partners. According to one study, when we start to think about finding a mate, men spend more on "status accessories" and women spend more on things that will make them look kind and caring.[4] Marketers are aware of these instincts and use them to their advantage through carefully constructed marketing. Of course, ads don't shout, "This will make you sexy!" Instead, they make associations between their brand and sexual dominance. It's as if they're letting us in on the secret of how to be successful. Our subconscious gobbles up all these clues. We might never openly admit to buying something to get a mate, but our subconscious will steer us to buy it anyway.

Through clever marketing, companies persuade us that we can become a better, higher-status version of ourselves with the click of a button and a credit card. And for our monkey brain, this is hard to resist. But resist we must. After all, no product genuinely has the power to make you cleverer, wealthier or more fun. This may seem obvious to your conscious self but your subconscious is more easily duped by marketing tactics. Therefore, repeat after me, as loud as possible without scaring people: "*No* product can make me a better or worse person." Whether I stripped you of everything you own or gave you all the products in the world, you would be the same you.

For those of us who know we use possessions as a crutch, Geoffrey Miller, author of *Must-Have: The Hidden Instincts Behind Everything We Buy*, offers reassurance by stating, "We humans have already spent millions of years evolving awesomely effective ways to display our mental and moral traits to one another through natural social behaviors such as language, art, music, generosity, creativity, and ideology."[5] So, while buying with one click on Amazon can feel easier than singing a song to our kids, discussing something interesting with a neighbor, or creating something, these are far better ways of scratching the itch that is our urge to show the world our value.

Fashion and status

"I'd rather cry in a Rolls-Royce than be happy on a bicycle."
—PATRIZIA (REGGIANI) GUCCI

It's not surprising that status-buying is most prevalent in fashion, as the clothes we wear are on display and immediately obvious. Fashion brands will go to great lengths to protect their status-giving ability. Hollister stores, owned by Abercrombie & Fitch, sell only up to size 6. Remarkably, this doesn't put people off but makes the products even more covetable to those who want to prove they're one of the "cool, skinny kids." Status is also behind the shocking reality that a large number of designer and high-end stores would rather burn or destroy their excess stock than discount it or donate it to charity. Brenda Polan from the London College of Fashion explains, "Most [brands] would be worried by the thought of a full-price customer on an expensive vacation to the developing world discovering that women of the shanty towns of Mombasa or Rio are wearing the same dress."[6]

Wow.

Let's hold it right there. Let's imagine the scene where this "full-price customer" goes to Mombasa and sees a poor woman wearing the same dress as her. What might happen?

The rich woman in the back of her luxury tour jeep looks across the dusty road. She squints, frowning, and then slowly pulls her designer sunglasses down her nose. There is a sharp intake of breath. The wiry local woman sweeping the dust away from her corrugated tin house is wearing this season's must-have pale green shift dress. What could it mean? The traveler feels her world crumble. She had been so proud of the dress and now she sees this slum-dwelling sweeper woman wearing the same thing! What's more, this woman looks rather better in it than she does. The meagerness of her diet means it doesn't pinch so much around the arms!

It almost feels as if having this designer dress doesn't make you special; doesn't make you worthier of admiration, love, and respect; doesn't make you better at all . . . why did she buy it in the first place?

Luxury brands won't let this happen because they are protecting their power to give their customers status. If, however, we buy using the principles of mindful curation, we won't have bought our clothes for status but for how they look and feel and perhaps to support a brand that has good values. Someone who has embraced the principles of a life less throwaway wouldn't feel scandalized because someone less wealthy than them was wearing the same thing. On the contrary, they'd smile and feel a kinship with that person. Lavish brands need to "protect their full-price customers" and keep their "exclusivity" purely to ensure they can continue charging the high prices that made them exclusive in the first place. However, I believe that our fragile egos and craving for status shouldn't be "protected" at the expense of our common humanity. Burner brands must do better if they don't want to be on the wrong side of history.

A note on fake designer products

After living in Hong Kong, I'm no stranger to fake goods, and I have been tempted to buy them. But now when I think about fake designer gear, I see it for what it really is: a fake attempt to show fake status. It might seem harmless enough, but by buying it you are still linking your self-esteem to an object, and a fake object at that. Would you wear a fake medal? If you believe in the values and quality of a designer brand enough to justify the price tag, then save up and invest in that brand in a legitimate way. It will mean that they can carry on doing what you believe in.

IF YOU WERE THE LAST PERSON ON THE PLANET

If everyone else on the planet disappeared, what would you wear? How would you live? What would be important to you and what would become unimportant? Really imagine it.

This will give you some insights into what you are really buying for yourself and what you might be buying to display your status.

I asked a couple dozen pals this very question. Almost all of them said they would dress purely for comfort, "a bit like when I was on maternity leave." A few said they would seek out quality tailoring and beautiful craftsmanship and continue to wear heels to lift their spirits, while others said they'd wear nothing at all! It's not evil to buy for others in society or for status (there's no way I'd wear my wedding dress in the apocalypse), but it's worth knowing that the reasons for buying and wearing certain things are external to you and you can choose to fight that if you wish.

How do you know if you're buying for status?

There are products that you buy for yourself that bring you pleasure—a cozy pair of slippers, a comfortable mattress, or a book you love. But then there are products that I believe we are really buying for other people, like a designer pair of heels or a flashy watch.

"What? They're for me too!" I hear you cry. How can we tell if we're buying for ourselves or for status? Try the thought exercise on the facing page.

Buying to prevent shame

A sizable amount of our status-buying is so we don't feel ashamed, left behind, or shown up by others. Shame, as horrible as it is, was a useful thing for early humans to develop. It prevents antisocial behavior such as stealing, fighting, or not using the toilet brush, and I'm all for that.

So shame has its place, but there are certain things we shouldn't feel ashamed about if we want to be free to make our own buying choices.

REFUSING TO FEEL ASHAMED

Write a list of things that you refuse to feel ashamed about when it comes to purchasing. To help you, here's my list. "I refuse to feel ashamed about . . ."

> Not having the latest gadget.
> Owning something that I like and others don't.
> Wearing the same outfit two hundred times.
> Giving my kids (if I'm blessed with a family) fewer physical things than other parents.

Say these pledges out loud to yourself (or to your cat, as I did, if you feel you need a witness). Remember these are

continued

conscious choices and you have good reasons for making them. Shame can be instinctual, so you need a strategy ready to deal with it when it arises.

To solidify this idea, you could even turn your "shame mantras" into "pride mantras." So mine would be "I feel proud that . . ."

> I am keeping something in use that would otherwise go to waste.
> I don't have to seek others' approval.
> I am happy with what I wear.
> I will be teaching my kids to value what they have.

Status and value—without buying

Status is so powerful that the higher our social position, the longer we'll live, regardless of our actual income. But here's the important part. Professor Michael Marmot, an expert on life expectancy, has discovered that it's what we *think* our status is that's important, not how others perceive us. If we feel valuable, worthy, and as good as anyone else, that works just as well as being Beyoncé.[7] We can't control others and we can't force them to give us a higher status, but we can control how we feel about ourselves. We could possibly grow our sense of self-worth by sitting on the couch and saying "I'm worth it" repeatedly, but earning our status by being a positive presence in others' lives will be a much more compelling argument to our subconscious.

We award the most value to the people who bring us joy, interesting information, help, advice, beauty, ideas, adventure, support, fun, and encouragement. And the good news is that we're all capable of doing this for others and being valued by them in return.

HOW TO INCREASE YOUR SENSE OF BEING VALUED BY YOUR TRIBE

It may require more energy than most of our favorite passive pastimes, but what has become clear in all the research that I've done is that it's the givers who are rewarded with the most happiness.

- Make a list of the people in your "tribe." Hint: The people you'd expect at your funeral.

- Make a list of ways in which you can have a positive impact on those people without neglecting yourself or hitting the shops. How can you add joy, interesting information, help, advice, beauty, ideas, adventure, support, fun, and encouragement? Be imaginative. Could you start a fun, new family tradition? Invent a silly secret handshake? Make time to call a relative regularly? Help declutter a pal's house? Surprise your lover? Take on responsibility for something. Take time to find out people's hopes and show you're behind them.

Whatever stage we're at in our lives and whatever our circumstances, we can be a positive influence on someone else's life and therefore be valued by them. We can be a poor, unwell person and still be revered for our stories, cheer, and wisdom, for sharing our own experiences in a helpful way and for making others feel better about what they're going through.

When you bring value to the lives of others, you will naturally feel more secure within your tribe. Your "status" will feel solid, so you'll feel less of a need to buy anything in an attempt to boost it.

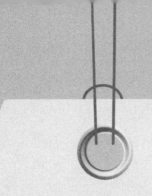

PART II

Living a
Life Less
Throwaway

7

Becoming a Curator

or
How to Begin Buying
with Purpose

Now that you've learned how to mute the manipulations of the marketers, you'll have the headspace to begin your curation journey. This starts with looking at what your priorities are not just for what you buy but for your whole life. That's right, we're going to be considering (cue capital letters) THE MEANING OF LIFE! It's going to get deep, but don't worry, I've stocked up on life vests and there's enough for everyone.

In our busy lives, we rarely take the time to step back and ask what it is that we want to bring to the world—what we can uniquely create. I don't mean in an artistic sense, but that purely by living your life, you create things. These could simply be a calm, safe environment for your family or joy and laughter in others. They *might* be award-winning art, but in my book (and this *is* my book) these creations are equal in value.

You might have a clear idea of your purpose already. If not, the following exercises will help you.

DIGGING DEEPER TO FIND PURPOSE

First, simply ask yourself how you want to touch your small corner of the world. What is most important that you create in your lifetime? Answer the following questions as quickly as possible, putting down the first thing that comes to mind.

- When did you last look up and find that time had flown by?

- What do you care about enough to be willing to take all the crap that comes with it?

- What did you care about as a child?

- What would you do if you knew you wouldn't fail?

- What would be worth failing at just to spend time doing it?

- What problems in the world do you think you could help with?

- What brings you strength and calm when you think about it?

DISCOVERING YOUR PASSIONS

This is more of a long-term exercise, but it's all the more revealing for being so, so please bear with it.

- Make a list of the top twelve things you want to do or try—hobbies, jobs, social activities, whatever. For example, some of mine would be writing, exploring, building a business, volunteering with kids, horse riding, connecting with friends and family, and campaigning for change.

continued

- Now assign a month of the year to focus on each of these in turn. Keep notes on how each makes you feel, both while you are doing the activity and in general. Examine why it makes you feel that way. For example, with horse riding it may be the feeling of freedom, the connection to an animal, the feeling of pride at being competent, or the sense of community that excites you.

- Look for the common threads between your passions and think about what that might reveal about your purpose, drives, and values.

KILL YOURSELF OFF (METAPHORICALLY)

Now I want you to write your own obituary. Yes, I went there, I'm sorry. But we know that death comes to us all and what's really important is to make the time we have on this crazy planet more meaningful. So, imagine you have died at the ripe old age of 101, and write a paragraph of your obituary from the point of view of a loved one and a paragraph from the point of view of someone in your work or a community you're involved in (or would like to be involved in in the future). What do you want them to say?

If this is too morbid for you, instead write your life story, including your future, in no more than a page. Start with "Once upon a time there was a . . . called . . . and they did something fantastic with their life" and go on to describe what happened.

BRINGING IT ALL TOGETHER

Now look back to identify what common threads and themes have come out of the previous three exercises. Even if you haven't started your experimental year, the activities you've thought of will give you an idea of what's important to you. Take some time and write down what you've found out about yourself.

Now use this to nail down five points that sum up your purpose, your mission statement. To give you an idea, this is mine:

- To follow my curiosity to experience as much of this spectacular world and the human ideas within it as I can.

- To be a positive force for this planet and its people.

- To use my creativity for art, books, and ideas.

- To foster deep connections and love with my chosen tribe.

- To create a nurturing and inspiring environment for my future family to thrive in.

I know that when I'm pursuing any of these things, I feel at home with myself. Your purpose can be tweaked as you find out more about yourself over the year, but because it's based on your core values and character, you should find it's reasonably stable over time.

If you can, put your mission statement somewhere where you can see it every morning. Change its position every now and again, so you don't get used to it. Do this until you know it by heart and it's sunk into your core.

YOUR PURPOSE AND YOUR PURCHASING

Now, when you think about purchasing something, ask yourself, "Does this object help me with my purpose?" The next chapter, where we take stock of all our belongings, is the perfect opportunity to really put this into practice. For example:

- *Sofa*—A comfy sofa allows me to connect with friends and family, therefore is purposeful.

- *A bigger TV*—The current TV works fine as a window of information and entertainment. A bigger one does not help me with any of my identified purposeful goals.

- *A sun hat*—This keeps me healthy as I experience the world, therefore is purposeful.

- *Five sun hats*—These create clutter and do not help my purpose.

- *A highly polluting car*—Creates experiences, but goes against my purpose toward the planet, therefore I should find a less-polluting alternative.

Future-proofing your purchasing

As with obsolescence, there are two sides to future-proofing: one physical and the other psychological. The physical, practical side of what to look for when buying different products is set out in Chapter 11, but the mental side is just as important.

Imagining the future is notoriously hard—just look at how wrong *Back to the Future Part II* got it. Ahem, flying cars? When? It's especially hard to predict our future tastes, though. Tastes can change drastically in early life. For example, I no longer yearn for a *Lion King* duvet cover, a Tamagotchi, or shorts that don't cover my whole behind. But from our late twenties onward, our taste tends to solidify and aspects of it can remain quite stable over our lifetime. Explore yours with the following exercise.

THE COMMON THREADS OF TASTE

To prevent regret and wasteful rebuying due to changes in taste, look at how your tastes have changed over the last ten years and see if there is anything that has stayed constant. In particular, look at:

- *Colors, textures, and patterns*—e.g., I love eggshell blue, bare wood, and lace but am not so keen on plastic.

- *Styles*—e.g., I love Craftsman houses, carved furniture, wrap dresses, and retro appliances.

- *Cultural influences*—e.g., I've faithfully loved Audrey Hepburn, period dramas, shabby chic, and café culture for the last fifteen years.

This exercise should help you be more mindful of your tastes while purchasing. If you can keep your main pieces in line with your more stable preferences, then, if you're really desperate to make a change, you can use smaller pieces to reflect your more "of the moment" inclinations.

BRAND VALUES—CAN BRANDS HELP US IN MINDFUL CURATION?

What's in a brand name? Would a Jo Malone candle by any other name smell as sweet? Branding originally started as an assurance of quality. It has been used for millennia. You can see loaves of bread from ancient Pompeii with a brand stamped into them showing the bakery they were baked in.

This kind of branding made sense. It meant that you could come to know which bakeries used the best flour, rather than chalk or dandruff.

Nowadays, however, while buying a particular brand is one of the most popular ways of expressing who we are, if we're trying to make decisions based on quality, the usefulness of the brand name has become muddied. This is because brand power has grown out of all proportion to quality. You can have two black T-shirts of the same size, same quality, and same cut, but one will sell for $7, the other for $35. The only difference is a little white smudge on the breast of one of them. As a dear friend said to me once, "The greatest magic trick of the modern age is to make people pay more for the same product just through branding."

Our old friend Christine Frederick noticed this phenomenon back in 1930, but she had a rather different take on it. Cue 1930s voice:

"You may place 500 words of perfectly clear laboratory analysis in front of a woman who is buying face powder, but she will still [buy] a French face powder of identically the same chemical composition, at twice the price, because she wants the French trade name to which someone through advertising has given value."[1]

Essentially, Frederick tells manufacturers not to bother informing shoppers about the details of their products but just to focus on the marketing, and then they can put up the prices regardless of whether the products actually are superior. This is of course exactly what millions of manufacturers went on to do.

Billions have been spent on branding and it's been so successful that seeing a brand logo actually, bizarrely, does make a difference in how we experience a product. In one experiment, 3- to 5-year-old children were given two sets of french fries and asked to describe how they tasted. The only

WHERE YOUR VALUES AND BRAND VALUES MEET

This exercise will help you apply the principles of mindful curation to the brands that you see every day.

- Write down your top six values. If you don't know what they are, imagine you're writing a list of values you'd like in a life partner—for example, integrity and dependability. These are what you should be looking for in a brand. (For a full list go to www.tarabutton.com/values.)

- Look at the brands you currently invest your money in. Do they meet your value criteria? (This might involve a little research.)

- If they fall short, ask them to do better (*see "Customer campaigning," following page*).

difference was that one set was packaged in plain wrapping and the other in McDonald's wrapping. Almost all the kids said that the McDonald's branded fries tasted better.[2] So the answer to the earlier question is that a rebranded Jo Malone candle *would* smell exactly the same, but we might very likely *think* it smelled less lovely if we were asked to compare it with a branded one. The brands that we love have the power to become part of our identity, and some research even suggests that when a brand we love is criticized, it lowers our own self-esteem. *Yikes!*

How to solve a problem like brands

It was shown by a research group in 2015 that we love some brands as much as we love our close friends.[3] I believe that we should make those businesses work harder to earn our love and respect through their products and service, not through the razzmatazz of their branding. What we don't want to do is act like a walking billboard for a company that doesn't back up its branding with genuine values.

Customer campaigning

Big brands have big followings, but that means we can demand more from them too. They're more likely to listen to customers and potential customers than outside activists. Use the #brandvalues hashtag. I'll get the ball rolling with this tweet to Apple:

> *Tara Button @tarabutton 5m*
>
> *@AppleSupport I'm a customer and I just want to urge you to consider the longevity in your products for the sake of the planet #brandvalues*

If there's a brand you'd like in your life (for its style, maybe) but you need the product to improve physically (perhaps to last longer) or be more ethical or sustainable to match your values, tell us at BuyMeOnce and we'll campaign to make it happen.

LEARNING TO COMMIT

Part of what this book aims to do is to help you better understand how products can meet your own particular needs, so you can commit wholeheartedly to things that will bring you joy for years to come. However, it's increasingly clear that we're losing our ability to commit. The fast pace of change and fear of missing out have turned us all into a load of flakes, always holding back in case something bigger and better comes along. So what should we do?

James Russell Lingerfelt, best-selling author of *The Mason Jar*, tells us that there are nine essential questions we should ask before committing to a person. I have borrowed them (with his kind permission) and made them relevant to products instead.

AN EXERCISE IN COMMITMENT

The next time you're about to buy something, use the following questions to help you decide whether to commit or not.

1. *How well do I know them?* (Have I done my research or could there be nasty surprises in store?)

2. *Can I trust them with my secrets?* (What is the brand's customer service and ethical record like?)

3. *Are we comfortable together in the quiet?* (Away from the seductive displays, will the product remain as attractive and interesting?)

4. *Do I know how this person will change me?* (Does the product align with who I am, or does it try to make me into something I'm not?)

5. *Am I attracted to their heart and character?* (Does the product hold any meaning for me past pure utility?)

6. *Do they appreciate me for who I am right now?* (Is this a product that can meet my immediate needs?)

7. *Are their hopes and dreams for the future compatible with mine?* (Is this a product that can meet my needs in the future?)

continued

8. *How do they already treat the people they love the most? (What do the reviews of this product say?)*

9. *Do they strive to place my desires and needs first? (Does the product help me express myself and my values, or does it mainly shout about itself?)*

Keep this list with you when you shop. Once you've chosen a product, commit to it. Have a mini-marriage in your mind:

"For better or worse, you're coming into my life and we're going to look after each other. You'll be reliable, and I won't swap you for the next hot model that comes along."

"I now pronounce you man and wi-fi-enabled TV."

Is anyone else tearing up?

BECOMING A STEWARD

No matter how much we buy, nothing that we have on Earth can be taken with us when we go, and we're here for such a short space of time. Our average life expectancy is around eighty years, while the life expectancy of many of our belongings is centuries long. However, we rarely think of this and the opportunity it presents to act as stewards for future generations.

Being a steward is both an act and a mindset. The act is simple. We buy things that are worthy of being handed down and made in a way that allows them to stand the test of time, and we take care of them over our lifespans with a view to passing them on. Even if an object doesn't end up with our own children, future generations can benefit from the choices we make now. Every decent product we buy will mean one less product in a landfill and one less product having to be made.

The *mindset* of a steward is more interesting to explore. When we think about future generations, our own ego is less involved. And we know that when we take our ego out of the equation, we tend to do things that make us truly happy. When we buy things and do things for others and with our community in mind, it nourishes us in a way that buying purely for ourselves doesn't. So, being a steward is another shield against materialism, and it's a way of forging a connection with those who will come after us.

The ancient Greeks had a wonderful saying, "A society grows great when old men plant trees whose shade they know they will never sit in." We should be planting ideas and objects that will nourish and shelter future generations. Through mindful curation we will be doing this in more ways than one. It's not just about leaving something for others, but leaving something *in* others, a sense of what we valued, what we cared about.

In three hundred years' time, the legacy of what you owned during your lifetime may still be alive and telling stories about who you were and what you cared about. Make sure your story is a good one.

8

Taking Stock
or
Where Did All This Stuff Come From?

Disney's *The Little Mermaid* might have been my first intro-
duction to a compulsive hoarder. She's constantly looking
for stuff that will make her feel part of a world she feels
excluded from. No matter how much she has, she wants
more. I think many of us relate to this in some way. If you
do have a house full of gadgets and gizmos aplenty, now's
the chapter to have a look at it all and see if it's serving you
well—and if not, let it go.

Clearing out possessions can sometimes feel wasteful.
However, I truly believe it's far more wasteful to keep possessions that are underused and underloved. All this excess does
is increase our stress levels and the time it takes to vacuum.
Plus, these things could be out doing good elsewhere, with
someone else who might need or love them.

Even if you're happy with the level of clutter in your house, I'd consider going through this stock-taking process because it's also an opportunity to discover your priorities, or to put them into practice, and plan how you might buy in a more meaningful way in the future.

If the idea of going through all your things is filling you with dread, take a deep breath. You can go at your own pace, and you'll feel very proud of yourself at the end of the process. Letting go of excess items can also give you a big boost in energy and a feeling of calm and freedom, which is a great way to start a new lifestyle. But first, a quick word about hoarding.

Hoarding

Around 5 percent of the population is affected by hoarding, which was recognized as a clinical condition in 2013, and it's useful to know the signs. I asked Lynne Drummond, one of the United Kingdom's leading hoarding experts, what the difference is between collecting and hoarding.

"It's a fine line," she said, "and one can merge into the other. With a collection, you know where everything is and you could find an item if you wanted to, whereas a hoard is just piles of stuff with no order to it. For me, collecting becomes hoarding when the things you have are stopping you from doing the things you want to do in your life. It's a sliding scale, of course, as with many situations.

"If you're helping a hoarder, be sensitive and remember that what looks like junk to you is really important to them. Once they've agreed to let an item go, remove it immediately, as the more an item is handled and the longer it stays in the house the harder it becomes to let go of. My message of hope to someone who suspects they are a hoarder and who feels trapped or ashamed by it is that there is help out there and you can change—it is possible. It may be difficult, but it can be done."

If you think you could be a hoarder, have an honest chat with your doctor about how it's affecting you, and ask to be referred to an expert who can help. If you just think you have a whole load of possibly unnecessary stuff in your house, read on.

Author's (rather bossy) note

Please hold off buying anything new while you're working through this chapter. Promise me (and yourself) that only food, toiletries, and cleaning products will go into your shopping cart. Right! Let's get to it.

THE LIFE-LESS-THROWAWAY CHALLENGE

My new pal Evan Zislis, author of *ClutterFree Revolution*, who has helped hundreds of people clear out, argues that in his experience, "most people truly love only about 20 percent of the stuff they possess. About 80 percent of their stuff they do not love. [So], about 80 percent of our space is occupied with storing everything else. Simplifying our stuff and refreshing our space is not as much about how we organize what we have as much as it is about loving what we keep."[1]

Imagine having only the things around you that you love, that you trust to work, and that you want to keep forever. How much more nourishing is that than piles of "well, I liked it in the shop" and "it will do for now?" This challenge is to help you find your 20 percent and is inspired by what minimalist Ryan Nicodemus put himself through in 2010. Ryan was a "successful" businessman chasing the

American dream who owned a huge number of things, including one hundred $100 ties. He was also desperately unhappy, unhealthy, and in debt. One day, with a help of a friend, he held a "packing party" and put absolutely everything he owned into carefully labeled boxes as if he was moving and then took things back out as he needed them. After Day 10, he didn't need to take out anything else; 80 percent of his possessions were still in the boxes so he sold or donated all of them.

You can re-create this challenge in your own life if you want to go hardcore, or try my modified challenge, which follows.

Modified Challenge

Packing up all your things might not be viable, especially if you live with others, so I've devised a workaround. It still requires effort and attention but doesn't require you to turn your whole life upside down. Block out some time to focus. This is especially important if you want other people in your household to get involved.

- Commit to taking a photo or putting a sticker on every item you use for the next two weeks. It will feel weird and inconvenient at first, but keep going. Set reminders on your phone if you keep forgetting.

- At the end, look at your collection of photos/ stickers. This is your A-team stuff—the swat team you need, no matter what. Now look around and notice what you haven't used. This will be important for the next stage, the actual decluttering.

Let's get tactical

It's very easy to drift about, nibbling at the edges of clutter. Therefore I've devised a strict list to follow. Checking off items as you go will give you a mini-bump of happy chemicals to keep you motivated. Each item has a space next to it so you can estimate the time it will take and schedule that time in your diary. You will need one bag/box each for recycling, landfill, donation, and items that need fixing.

Start small

Go for an easy win first. I strongly suggest starting with your underwear drawer. Find every bra, pair of socks, tights, panties, and boxers in the house, even the ones in the laundry; put them all together in one place; and decide which ones deserve to go back in the drawer. Here are the rules; there are only two:

1. Keep only the items you'd be happy to reach for first.

2. No one needs more than two weeks' worth of underwear.

Everyone has a bunch of "not quite right" pieces that sit in the back of the drawer waiting for the glorious day that all the others are in the wash. This may sound slightly fascist but you must reject these weaklings. I suggest you have nothing but A-team underwear. Soft, comfortable, attractive, and right for the occasions that you need them. These are the items you reach for first when everything is washed. Pay attention to each item. Have a little feel. If you don't like its texture, it's gone. If you like it but there's a hole in it, put it in a fixing pile to be dealt with at the end of this process.

Put all rejected underwear straight into a fabric recycling bag and put it by your door ready to be taken away. Some may also be used as cloths and dusters.

Now admire your A-team. They deserve to be stored well. If you take care of them, they'll take care of your privates.

Arrange them so you can see everything at once when you open your drawer. A couple of shoeboxes can be perfect for separating sports socks from dress socks or bras from tights. I use the Marie Kondo method of folding instead of balling. This way, all my items are folded into little parcels and sit up beautifully in ranks.

If someone had told me last year that I'd get pleasure from folding my underwear, I'd have given them my best raised eyebrow. But I tried it, and I'm hooked. The sense of peace and relief when I don't have to rummage or make do with odd socks makes the minute of folding time completely worth it. I also managed to get three drawers of underwear down to one, which gave me the confidence to move on to the next challenge.

The formula

This is the formula that you will now use for the rest of your things.

Keeping:

- Gather everything together.

- Examine or try on each item, but not for too long. If you can't decide what to do with it in 1 minute, it goes.

- Find your A-team items.

  - The ones you always call on first.

  - The ones you can see yourself using long into the future.

  - The ones that make you happiest.

  - Take a moment to be grateful for these core items. Focusing on what you're keeping will help soothe you as you let other items go.

- Beyond your core items, make sure everything really works hard to justify its place. If you're unsure, err on the side of getting rid of it.

- Duplicates or items that perform the same function can go unless they are part of a set or "work uniform" you wear or use regularly. If not, keep the better one.

- Sort the leftover items into the fix, recycle, or donate boxes. Very little should become landfill.

- If you have A-team items that you're saving for "best," start using them. Don't be the person who goes to their grave with unused wedding china.

Reasons not to keep things if you're not sure:

- It was expensive.

- It was a gift.

- I feel I *should* like it.

- I want to fit into it again.

- A friend once complimented me on it.

Storing:

Store items so that you can see them and access them easily. Every item or group of like items should have a designated place. Partitions and labels are your friends here.

The categories

Clothing

Finding your A-team capsule wardrobe (see page 90) frees you from that "nothing to wear" feeling and allows you to see what you really care about when it comes to your style. Here's your challenge checklist. Good luck!

CATEGORY	TIME AND DATE COMMITTED	DONE
Bags		
Bottoms and skirts		
Care products for clothing		
Dresses and suits		
Hats, scarves, and gloves		
Other accessories (sunglasses, umbrellas, belts, and ties)		
Shoes		
Sleepwear (including robes)		
Sportswear		
Tops, jackets, and coats		
Underwear		
Uniforms		

Grooming and health products

This is where duplicates play a huge role. You do not need seven half-filled bottles of shampoo. Imagine you're going on a two-week vacation. Pack what you need to make you feel good. The rest will have to fight for their right to stay.

CATEGORY	TIME AND DATE COMMITTED	DONE
Hairdryers, brushes, combs, and curlers		
Makeup, nail care, and perfume		
Medicine and first-aid kit		
Personal hygiene products		
Shaving equipment and products		
Toothcare, skincare, and washing products		

Housewares

This is a huge section, but many of the pieces are large and one-off, so will naturally stay. As you go through, notice the ones that have worn well and stayed in tune with your personal sense of style. This will be invaluable when it comes to buying new things when needed. Also, pay particular attention to how you use your furniture. Is all of it used? Are your decorative pieces actually looked at? If not, can they go or can they be given more prominence?

CATEGORY	TIME AND DATE COMMITTED	DONE
Bed linen, towels, washcloths, and dusters		
Curtains, cushions, throws, and rugs		
Furniture		
Figurines, vases, clocks, candles, and other non-sentimental ornaments		
Lamps, plants, and mirrors		

Kitchenware

Kitchenware tends to be easier, as it's all pretty functional. Just remember to keep things for the life you actually have. If you don't make muffins on a regular basis, you don't need seven muffin trays. Use this opportunity to ask yourself questions about the future. Is muffin making something you want in your future life? These kinds of questions might seem trivial but they actually give us a chance to assess our priorities in life. Remember that some equipment is easily borrowed and that gives you an opportunity to connect with your neighbors.

CATEGORY	TIME AND DATE COMMITTED	DONE
Cutlery and crockery		
Large appliances		
Laundry accessories (iron, etc.)		
Pet products		
Pots and pans		
Small appliances		
Storage		
Utensils		

Technology

Old technology haunts many a house. You'll be surprised at how much you might get for it if you sell it, although make sure you take your data off any computer you pass on. Go through everything before you throw out that "mystery cable" or it'll be the one thing needed to make your camcorder work. Fix whatever can be fixed that you will use again, and, please, whatever you do, don't put any of it in the trash. Consider giving old items to people who might use them. Recycle, freecycle, donate, or upcycle.

Also, future-proof any technology you keep by storing the manuals, warranties, and spare parts in a designated place.

CATEGORY	TIME AND DATE COMMITTED	DONE
Cables and chargers		
Cameras and recorders		
Computers, modems, and routers		
Phones and MP3 players		
Printers and faxes		
TVs and DVD players		
Wearable tech		
Other gadgets		

Hobbies

If you're anything like me, you've spent much of your life jumping from hobby to hobby, buying all the supplies and then losing interest. If you truly believe you'll get back into knitting or kite-surfing, give yourself a time limit within which to do so. After that, the items get donated.

CATEGORY	TIME AND DATE COMMITTED	DONE
Books and magazines		
Care products for equipment		
Craft equipment		
DIY equipment		
Games and toys		
Seasonal decorations		
Sports equipment		
Other hobbies		

Memories and jewelry

This is a tricky category because the sentiment tied up with jewelry, even cheap costume items, is hard to ignore. I wear only four pieces and I'm happy for these to be the only jewelry I own, but you'll have to be honest with yourself over how many baubles you will wear regularly.

Consider making a work of art or decor out of sentimental but unworn jewelry. Find a way of displaying these pieces, sell them, or pass them on to others, but *don't* put them back in a drawer. I have many little boxes of jewelry from various godparents, aunts, and uncles. I don't wear any of it, but it feels heartless to sell it, so it has sat in a drawer for three and a half decades. I've now decided to take these pieces, along with my mother's notes describing whom they're from, and display them on a jewelry tree as a symbol of my family and the love and support they've given me. This idea need not just apply to jewelry. If there's anything in your life that feels particularly emotional or precious but spends its time in a box, try to find a way to bring it into the light. An unused and unseen object is a wasted object. It is merely a thing you possess, and that isn't enough to justify its place in your life.

Family heirlooms connect us to our past and our identity, however, so it can be worth keeping particularly special, valuable, or historically interesting pieces to pass on to children and grandchildren. If you find yourself awash with sentimental trinkets, though, choose one to keep that can symbolize a group of them.

CATEGORY	TIME AND DATE COMMITTED	DONE
Jewelry		
Paper memorabilia— cards, letters, and so on		
Photographs and diaries		
Sentimental ornaments and memorabilia objects		

What you're left with

Once you've gone through everything and put the items you're sure you want to keep back in their designated space, you may be left with some "stuff to use someday" and "stuff to fix someday." The way to deal with these is to make "someday" a particular day.

"Stuff to use someday" (e.g., gym equipment)

These items should be given a chance, but a time-restrictive chance. Give them a "use-by date" six months, one year, or, in exceptional circumstances, two years away. If they haven't been used by then, they go. Put a reminder in your calendar on those dates, and on a date one month before, to warn you that these things are about to "expire." If you want to justify their presence in your home, they must pull their weight and you must get into the habit of using them. I imposed a deadline of one year to start regularly playing the keyboard crammed in my living-room closet. Wish me luck.

"Stuff to fix someday"

Quite simply, get it all together and block out a "fixing week" when you'll take it to be fixed. If you're hoping to fix it yourself, give yourself a time limit. If you haven't done so within a couple of weeks, either take it to a professional, bribe a handy friend with baked goods, or let it go. (*For more on repairing, see Chapter 12 and Appendix I.*)

KEEPING OUT THE CLUTTER

Some people are born with too much stuff, some people acquire too much stuff, but many people have too much stuff thrust upon them. What should we do when we suddenly inherit or are given things?

Presents

In the past, when I received a present I didn't like, I thanked the person profusely, put the gift in a random drawer where it remained for a year or two, until I felt it had "done its time," and then agonized over giving it away. Nowadays, I still thank the person profusely, however, if it's from someone I can be candid with, I'll tell them it's not quite right and ask if it can be exchanged for a similar object that I will use. If the unwanted present is from someone who would be upset if I asked for the receipt, I thank them profusely and give the present straight to charity. It will be far better off being used by someone else than sitting in my dusty drawer for the next year.

Some might feel this is wasteful or ungrateful and let the guilt stop them, but I believe it's more wasteful to have an object sitting there not being used. And you can still be grateful that a friend or loved one took the time to think of you. Once they have given their gift, they will have got what they wanted out of the exchange too—to feel thoughtful and kind toward you—so it's a win-win situation.

A strategy for presents

To maximize the chances of being given presents you'll love and use, you could give your family and friends a wish list. If this works for you, it can certainly solve a lot of issues. Rather awkwardly, I prefer to be surprised. Asking family to do a secret Santa can reduce the overall number of presents, and asking them for a special day together rather than a physical object can be very rewarding. If you work in a position where you tend to receive lots of little gifts, maybe request a donation in your name instead. If you are an elementary school teacher, you can send a note home with the kids suggesting classroom supplies instead of saying that you don't need gifts at all.

The best way to get your family and friends to buy you presents that both reflect your style and values and last a long time is to involve them in your goal to live a life less throwaway. Lend them this book, talk about mindful curation, and explain that you now want to only bring things into your life that will remain there to be treasured. Be clear about what your values are when it comes to products, what styles you like, and what you actually need in your life. Since

I've begun this lifestyle, my family has changed the way they give me gifts. I now receive many more experiences, and any material objects are things that I both need and that will last, because they know this is important to me.

So, dear family, if you're reading this, well done. I didn't give away any of my Christmas gifts this year!

Inherited items

Immediately after a loved one's death, everything down to the disposable razors in their bathroom can feel precious. It is also a very overwhelming and emotional time, which makes it doubly hard to make clear decisions about what to do with physical items. Once you start to go through the sheer number of things that one person accumulates over their lifetime, though, you soon start to become more pragmatic. Even so, you can easily find yourself swamped by an influx of things that you want to "keep in the family" or "don't want to waste."

It's easier said than done, but do try to keep only the things that make sense to add to your life. You may want to keep one or two items that were particularly memorable to you growing up, so that your own children and grandchildren might have that connection to their past. Pass other items on to a place where they can fulfill their destinies as useful or beautiful objects and bring someone else joy. Remember that one object can hold just as much power as one hundred when it comes to memories, and take photographs of rooms before clearing them.

When it comes to letting things go, harsh as this may sound, don't let the deceased's attitude to their own things cloud your judgment. It may be that "Grandpa would hate to see these sold," but if the alternative is to cram your home with things you don't like or use, they should be sold, or donated, or passed to other members of your family. If it eases your conscience, give the proceeds of the sale to a charity or a cause your loved one supported.

A strategy for the division of objects

When relatives of mine died, my family put together a very civilized system of deciding who would keep what, and it worked well. So I'm offering it here, as it may be a helpful strategy for you during a difficult time.

- First, take an inventory of every major item. This is a long process. However, it can be done by taking pictures and creating a gallery instead of writing it all down.

- Then, next to each object, have family members mark 1, 2, or 3, meaning:

  1. I would really love to have this.

  2. If no one else desperately wants this, I'd like it.

  3. I'm not desperate for this, but I feel it should stay in the family.

This takes some of the emotion out of the process. You'll find that hopefully not too many items are wanted desperately by several people. When there are disputes, the list can be used to help resolve them, for example, "We both really want these four items. Why don't you take two, and I take two?

From taking stock to stocking up

The stock-taking exercise in this chapter will have taken you on a real journey. What's important now, as with any journey, is to remember what you learned about yourself along the way and to use this knowledge in your life going forward. Look for the patterns in what you kept and what you threw away and take notes. These notes will help you with the next stage of living a life less throwaway, which is to only "stock up" on the things you believe you can commit to and will have in your life for the foreseeable future.

9

Before You Shop

or
A Tale of Two Shoppers

Most of us spend more time shopping than we do socializing, and the average woman will spend more than four years of her life buying something or other.[1] There are many different types of shopper, but they can be roughly split into the *impulse shopper* and the *mindful shopper*. Retailers love an impulse shopper because they're easy to manipulate, swayed by trends and promotions, and fear missing out, so they spend more. A mindful shopper, on the other hand, takes their time and knows what they like and what they will like in the future. They're savvy enough to see past the manipulations of the retail world and so make purchases on their own terms.

If you have impulse-shopping tendencies, as I once did, this chapter will help you kick those habits and empower you with tips and techniques that you can use both at home and when shopping. This may be jarring at first, but a small amount of effort now will lead to big rewards in the future—less debt, less buyer regret, less clutter, and less stress. I aim to make mindful shoppers out of all of you who have put your time and trust in this book.

THE POWER OF THE UNWISH LIST

More than a year ago, I wrote what became one of the most popular articles on the BuyMeOnce website. It was a personal list of things I didn't need, an "unwish" list. And I encouraged others to do the same. I knew that it had been a useful exercise for me, but I didn't realize quite how much of an impact it would have on others until they started writing in, with some professing it was both liberating and life-changing.

Things I don't need

When I was growing up, accumulating things seemed like a rite of passage to adulthood. The choice between having and not having something was a no-brainer to me. I *always* wanted the thing. My constant refrain while out shopping was "But Mummy, I need it! I *need* it!" And I believed this. I couldn't distinguish between wanting and needing—I felt that I needed everything. And it's easy for this mindset to continue, with the only thing holding back the purchase being how much money is in your bank account. So, I've made a list of "things I don't need" to remind myself that no matter how much I have to spend, I do not need everything offered.

My "unwish" list

Kitchen

> I do not need gadgets like bread machines or waffle
>   makers.
> I do not need more than four pots and one frying pan.
> I do not need matching mugs.

Clothes and accessories

> I do not need a watch.
> I do not need any more than eight pairs of shoes.
> I do not need more than a capsule wardrobe.

Technology

I do not need a gaming console.
I do not need a desktop computer.
I do not need any DVDs.
I do not need GPS.

Furniture

I do not need any more throw pillows.
I do not need friends' freebies that don't fit in my home.
I do not need decorative knickknacks that have no
   meaning to me.
I do not need any seasonal decor (e.g., Halloween
   cushions).

Leisure

I do not need any musical instruments other than my
   guitar and piano.
I do not need any more gym equipment.
I do not need any magazines (unless work related).
I do not need any massage/exfoliation/pampering
   gadgets.
I do not need any more cat toys.

Beauty

I do not need any makeup other than my staple five
   (concealer, mascara, eye shadow, blush, and lip
   balm).
I do not need any hair products other than shampoo,
   conditioner, and serum.
I don't need any nail care other than clippers, file, polish
   remover, and my favorite color polish.

Stationery

I do not need any more pens or pencils.

I *really* don't need more notebooks.

I do not need anything further to help organize my stationery.

I do not need any cute sets of paper clips, mini-highlighters, etc.

I should stress that this is just the list of things that I *personally* don't feel I need. It may be that a Halloween cushion would bring you never-ending joy and happiness, in which case get one immediately.

WRITE YOUR OWN UNWISH LIST

Use the previous categories to make your own unwish list. Feel free to go into more detail than I did for the categories in which you often impulse-buy. Don't be tempted to do this in your head; make sure you process it properly by taking the time to think about it and write it down. Send it to yourself as an e-mail so that it's backed up, and set a reminder in your calendar to review it every few months to see if you've stuck to it and if there's anything you might want to add.

Here's a tip: If there's a product that you tend to impulse-buy regularly, remind yourself how many lovely things you already own by displaying them all together in one place, as they might be in a store, and taking a picture. Then, when you get tempted while out and about, you can think back to your own "shop" at home and leave the store empty-handed, happy in the knowledge that you already have enough. I did this with notebooks and it worked great!

A FEW THINGS TO DO BEFORE
HITTING THE STORES

It's good to prepare and contemplate before you go shopping. Below are some ways to do this.

Think differently about possessions

It's often helpful to think less about our possessions and more about *the results* we want from having those possessions. For example, we don't need a washing machine; we need clean clothes. We don't need to own a washing machine to achieve this. We may have a laundromat close by, or be able to send out our clothes, if such a service is available in our area. Some other examples:

- We may not need a car. We do need to get around easily.

- We may not need a TV. We do need something fun and relaxing to do in the evening.

- We may not need to own tools or books. We do need access to them.

- We may not need a particular brand of dress/suit. We do need to be able to go where we want and feel happy in what we're wearing.

In each case, there may be a better way to get the result we need than buying something new. If, after thinking about this, you still know you want to buy a product, then it's about making sure that product is the best one for you long term.

Research

Start your research with a quick look at Chapter 11, and see if there is any advice there on the product you're considering. Then do any further digging you might need. Who can you trust when researching?

- Trust yourself! If you can borrow the product and try it before you buy it, that's best of all.

- Trust friends' recommendations if you trust their judgment (but get a few opinions if you can).

- Trust independent reviewers such as *Consumer Reports* and the Good Housekeeping institute.

- Trust magazines and bloggers to a certain extent. Look for reviews where a few products are being compared to each other; they tend to be more critical and discerning and are less likely to be advertorials.

- Trust salespeople for certain facts, but not necessarily for their opinions.

Make a list of your needs and the criteria for your product and then go armed with that list to the store.

Purchasing from a position of strength

You want to come to a purchase from a position of strength. In the same way that you should never go food shopping while you're hungry, don't go clothes or home decor shopping to feed an emotional hunger. You'll buy things to bolster your ego rather than serve yourself.

Before you shop, spend a second assessing your current state of mind. Are you feeling solid and whole, or is there any anxiety or insecurity there? If you do sense that your drive to shop is coming from a negative place, do this quick exercise. It's designed to give you a quick boost of self-esteem, in the same way that you might eat a banana before you go grocery shopping.

Purchase with planning

Always have a list when you go shopping, even if it's only one item long and even if it's nonspecific—for example,

NOURISHING YOUR SELF-ESTEEM

When you accept yourself unconditionally, showing off to the world or making up for perceived flaws by owning things becomes miraculously less important.

- Close your eyes and think about someone who loves you just as you are, who wouldn't change their feelings for you whether you were wearing Prada or a plastic bag.

- Imagine yourself in their body, looking at yourself through their eyes. Feel those feelings of love, respect, kindness, and empathy. Direct them toward yourself and feel their warmth. Tell yourself you accept yourself unconditionally.

- Try to hold on to these feelings as you shop.

"something I can wear to formal summer occasions." Don't stray from that list and don't add to it while you're shopping. If you're tempted by something off-list while you're out, take a picture of it and consider it outside of the bewitching shopping environment.

Purchase with patience

Of everything I've found hard to conquer on my mindful-curation journey, impatience has been the hardest. Once I've decided that I want something, I find it very hard not to get it immediately. This can lead to buying "not quite the right thing" just because it's available right away. Impatience is a virtue from the point of view of people trying to sell us stuff. But learning to delay gratification is necessary if we want to practice mindful curation.

Set yourself a rule that for any purchase over a certain amount, you have to wait twenty-four hours to "authorize it" to yourself. Put it on your wish list but don't buy it until the next day. This should leave you enough time to raise any objections in your mind, and it helps break the addictive cycle of impulse shopping.

Of course, if you're in a physical store, it may not be practical to come back the next day. So, if you can delay your purchase for a week, do that instead. If not, at the very least, leave the shop and walk around the block before making the purchase. If you're looking for a product and can't find something that checks all your boxes, instead of grabbing any old thing, try these other options.

- Tell the manufacturer your needs. There may be something new coming along.

- Rank the criteria you've set from most important to least important and use that to make a choice that compromises your needs as little as possible.

- If money is the biggest issue, put some money aside each month until you can pay for it.

- If it can't wait, and you think you can pay the money back within a year, find finance at a reasonable rate and work out a plan for repayment.

- If you can't pay for it within a year, or without putting a strain on your income, go back to ranking the criteria you've set and find a product you can afford.

HOW TO AVOID IMPULSE BUYING

Remember that Haribo advertisement with the children who had to resist the sweets laid out in front of them (page 59)? What's interesting (and slightly ironic) is that this ad was based on a real 1960s experiment about willpower. It is now commonly known as the "Marshmallow Test." It found that the kids who resisted a marshmallow in order to win another one ended up with better SAT scores, were slimmer, and had more of a sense of self-worth in the future.[2] Being able to delay gratification for a bigger prize in the future seems to be the key to many of the things we want—so all those Haribo kids failed!

I don't believe we are born with a certain amount of willpower. The kids who did well in the original test all had strategies to make the temptation easier to bear. Some turned the chair around and sat with their back to the sweet, some sang songs to themselves, and some pushed the sweet away. These were all simple and childish solutions, but they worked. Also, when the kids were *given* a strategy to resist the treat, they did so much more easily, so it's not just about how you're born.

With that in mind, we need to come up with strategies to prevent impulse buying. Our willpower gets used up each day making tough decisions, focusing on tricky tasks, and resisting unhealthful food. The temptation terrorists only need to get lucky once to screw up our best intentions, and being vigilant all the time can be exhausting. The best way to preserve willpower is to form anti-impulse habits that then run automatically and without effort. Following are ideas on how to do that.

Identify times of temptation

First, you must identify the times and places where you get tempted. Is the superstore your downfall? Is Amazon your doom? Go through your bank statements and see where you're spending your money. Pay particular attention if any of the entries give you a twinge of regret or guilt. Ask yourself whether you can avoid the tempting area completely. It may not be the actual shopping you're addicted to but the beauty of the store or the sense of going somewhere. Feed these needs in more positive ways, like going to an exhibition or arranging to meet friends at times you might usually shop.

If you can't avoid the places where you are triggered, try to distract yourself in some way while you're there. Get into the habit of calling a friend as you walk past the stores, or try to remember everything you wrote on your unwish list. Interestingly, with everyone looking at their phone while waiting in checkout lines nowadays, impulse buys such as chocolate have gone down drastically.[3] So distracting yourself works, but you may have to *plan* to be distracted. If you tend to get sidetracked and purchase *additional* things when shopping for essentials online, set up Freedom on your computer to cut out the internet after fifteen minutes, so that you have to focus on getting the items you need quickly and won't drift into your own cave of Wonderbras or gadgets.

If items pop up that you're interested in, add them to a wish list instead of a cart. Then give yourself a specific day, maybe the first of the month, when you go through your wish lists and mindfully assess each product. Will it help you with your life's purpose? Is it the best product for the result you need? Is it something you can commit to? Can you see it fitting into your life in a decade's time?

Habits and triggers

Bad habits such as impulse shopping happen because our brains are trying hard to be helpful by saving us energy and doing certain tasks itself. So when it recognizes a scenario, say, going past McDonald's, and knows what usually happens next, it goes on autopilot. It switches off the part that makes

IDENTIFYING IMPULSE-BUYING TRIGGERS

The most effective way to overcome a habit is to identify its trigger and replace that with something else.

- Write down what triggered your last five impulse purchases. What were you doing just before? What were you thinking? Who were you with? Can you see a pattern of behavior?

- How can you prevent the trigger from resulting in spending? Can you avoid going to that place/website, or change your routine in some way? Disrupting your habit trigger even just a little bit can do the trick.

- Review in six months. Did it work? If not, is there something else you can try?

conscious decisions, the cerebral cortex, and runs completely on the basal ganglia. This is one of the deepest parts of the brain, a place your conscious thoughts can't access, and so the next thing you know, you're holding a hot apple pie. This habit forming works well for brushing our teeth every morning, but less well when it causes us to sleepwalk into buying a treat every time we go past McDonald's.[4]

ADVICE FOR HIGH-MAINTENANCE PURCHASES

Knowing whether to buy something that will involve a lot of upkeep and commitment is a classic problem. One excellent solution for this was proffered on a 2005 TV show called *Ann Widdecombe to the Rescue*. In one episode, Ann came across a family where the young son was desperate for a puppy and insisted he would be responsible for it, but the parents didn't believe him. Ann's advice was that he should be given a hamster. If after six months he had looked after it all by himself, he could be given a dog. The parents agreed, a hamster was purchased, and Ann returned to the house six months later. To the parents' obvious surprise, their son had kept to the bargain, diligently tending to his furry potato of a pet, and he was then rewarded with the puppy he'd dreamed of.[5]

Many of us (me included) act like kids when it comes to high-maintenance objects. We promise ourselves we'll do the upkeep, but after a few enthusiastic maintenance sessions (shoe polishing, rubbing oil into chopping boards, pan seasoning), we get lazy. If you want to buy a high-maintenance object but aren't sure you'll follow up with the necessary care, train yourself to do the maintenance first and *then* buy yourself the object as a reward. Pick something that you already have, such as a pair of shoes, and set yourself the task of polishing them once a week. If you do it for six weeks, you can treat yourself to your high-maintenance leather jacket. This might seem rather crazy in a world where we want the things we want when we want them (which is always *now*), but this due-diligence period is useful. You won't be buying on impulse, and you'll enjoy the anticipation of waiting for the product to come into your life. Keeping the small promise of maintaining an object also boosts your self-trust and self-esteem.

Sometimes it can be tempting to buy for a fantasy person you'd like to be—someone who has time to polish silver and dust chandeliers. We might even buy something in the hope that the purchase will magically transform us into that diligent person. Trust me, it doesn't work.

GETTING IT TO STICK

If you feel motivated to become a mindful shopper, consider teaching a friend how to become one. This isn't a sneaky ploy to get you to talk about my book to others—it has been proven that if we teach others the things that we want to remember ourselves, we have a much higher chance of being able to recall them.[6] So, in the next few hours, pick someone you think might be interested and tell them as much as you can remember about the tactics outlined in this chapter. Skim the chapter again if necessary to see how much of it has sunk in. You might be surprised how well this works.

10

Out at the Shops

or

How Scents, Shelves, and Salespeople Get Us Spending

"The odds of going to the store for a loaf of bread and coming out with only a loaf of bread are three billion to one."
—ERMA BOMBECK

We may go into stores with the intention of shopping mindfully but by the time we've left, many of those intentions have been cleverly unpicked. We know that 50 percent of purchases are on impulse.[1] So what happens in there? This chapter will reveal all the tricks of the retail world and how we can dodge their little games, beat the system and bring home the BuyMeOnce bacon without a basket of this and that.

THE SNEAKINESS OF RETAIL

The longer you stay in a store, the more money you will spend, so shops and shopping centers are designed to make it as hard to leave and as tempting to stay as possible. IKEA turns its stores into mazes so that even if you only came in for a chair, it's almost impossible not to end up with a cartload of twinkle lights, planters, and storage solutions.

Store layout

Both supermarkets and stationery stores, my personal downfall, will put their most common items, such as milk or printer paper, at the very back, forcing us to walk past everything else. Thankfully, there are some very simple ways to get around these manipulations. Make a list and stick to it. Allow yourself to browse if you're actively looking for inspiration, but if you see something that looks interesting, take a photo of it with your phone to review it later rather than buy it there and then.

Online stores use slightly different tactics. They bring our attention to things that we *weren't* shopping for by letting us know that "other customers who bought that also looked at this," and pairing items with something we're already buying. If something else does pique your interest, add it to a wish list to consider later, but don't stray from what you planned to buy.

Extra tip: A big shopping cart makes you buy more, because it doesn't look full. If you're looking to save money, pick up a smaller cart or basket instead.

Visual marketing

Seventy-six percent of people don't talk to salespeople,[2] so stores use "visual merchandising" to sell us a vision or tell us a story and steer us toward the things they want us to impulse-buy. These stories can be very seductive. "Would you like to be a whimsical, romantic creature who trips through meadows and drinks tea from mismatched vintage crockery? You can be that person if you buy this dress, this cup, this Polaroid camera. . . ." The most common story is simply "I'm a cool, confident, attractive person." This is what mannequins' body language has been designed to express. Because thinness has come to symbolize success in our society, some mannequins are also so thin that their spines and shoulder blades jut out and their ribs are exposed. They are designed to "outrank" us in this way and make us want what "they have."

To counter this, we need to be really clear about what our own story is and what we want it to be *before* entering a shop. If you haven't already done them, the exercises in Chapters 5 and 7 can help.

Scent and music

Certain smells are very powerful and can trigger all sorts of mischief in our brain—anyone who's ever experienced smelling something and getting a powerful flashback will know this. This has, of course, been exploited by marketers. A 2006 study showed that when the scent of vanilla was added into the air of a store, sales of women's clothing *doubled*.[3] Particular scents put us in a relaxed, excited, or happy mood that rubs off on the objects we see, making us feel we like them more than we really do.

Music works in a similar way. It lifts our mood, making us more likely to spend. Slower music makes us slow down as we walk around the aisles, and classical music can even make us buy more expensive items.

These are both good reasons why doing your research in advance and implementing a 24-hour cooling-off period are a good idea, or looking in-store and then buying the items online once you've had the chance to think.

Packaging

Packaging can distract or mislead us about the product itself—just think of eggs from caged hens in boxes showing happy chickens strolling on grassy fields. Your focus should always be on what's inside the packaging, because that is where the real product benefit is.

At my local vet's office, there was a tub full of dog bones on the front desk over Christmastime. The receptionist said that they had hardly sold any until she added a ribbon to each one. Within a couple days, they had sold out. I found this startling and the moral I've taken away is to buy for the bone, not for the ribbon. A ribbon does not make a bone any juicier.

Product information

Too much information given all at once can also be used to bamboozle us to the point where we lose our will to compare products properly and buy impulsively. One thing to watch out for particularly are products that shout about the one feature that beats the competition. This tactic can be used to make us feel that this feature is more important than all the others.

But, like a person who only has a picture of their abs on their dating profile, it's important not to be distracted from what matters to you. If abs are all that you care about in a partner, then by all means you should go for ab-man/woman, but generally you might have a few more criteria to consider. My husband has only one ab, but he comes with all the other "product features" I decided were important to me in a life partner. Decide which features and criteria are important to you in advance, so you don't get hoodwinked.

Loyalty cards and gamification

There was a time when my whole wallet was so stuffed with loyalty cards, I couldn't close it. Loyalty schemes can be advantageous, but they do come at a price. We can end up giving away more information than we realize, including what we might be tempted into buying in the future.

A famous case published in the *New York Times* told of an angry father who called up Target's head office demanding to know why they were sending his teenage daughter coupons for maternity clothes and diapers. Target apologized, but a couple of days later the company received an apology from the father, saying, "it turns out there have been some activities in my house I haven't been completely aware of. She's due in August."[4] Yes, Target had gotten so good at tracking their customers' shopping habits, they could tell if someone was pregnant before her family did. Target soon found that their activities were creeping out their customers, though, so they got subtler about it, putting baby product coupons in among other items. "We found out that if a pregnant woman thinks she hasn't been spied on, she'll use the coupons," said one Target statistician. Well, that's not creepy at all!

Other brands use different tactics. Samsung increased visits to its website by 66 percent when it turned its loyalty scheme into a game where you could earn points, unlock and collect badges, and boost your rankings.[5] Tapping into our competitive and playful nature is an easy way for brands to get us to engage with them.

If a brand both meets your needs and matches your values, then by all means take advantage of its loyalty program. Just make sure that you go into it or obtain a store card knowing that it will come with additional pressures to spend. Use the "Would I still need it if it was full price?" rule when shopping with coupons or a discount. At the end of the day, stores have these offers to make you spend more. And the store almost always wins, but it won't if you're practicing the tactics of mindful curation.

Pester power: kids at stores

The average American parent spends $371 a year on toys per child.[6] Our children are perhaps the best salespeople of all. They have the persuasive patter, including the threat of having a meltdown in the Tonka Truck aisle if they don't get what they've set their hearts on. One of the best ways to reduce the pressure to buy your kids things is to reduce the amount of advertising they're exposed to (see Chapter 4). But when it comes to taking them on a physical shopping trip, it's all about setting expectations before you go out. If you are going to buy them something, let them know in advance that it will be one toy, or that it will be within a certain budget. This is also a great opportunity to teach them about the value of money, so be sure to let them know how many weeks' pocket money it is they'll be spending.

Also, implement a one-in one-out system, where if a child wants a new toy they have to first pick one to donate. Before you go shopping for the toy together, ask the child which old toy they are going to part with. This will automatically make them more mindful of what they decide to buy. They might even decide they don't want anything enough to give up something, and this is okay too. They shouldn't ever feel pressured into buying something new. Always give them the choice of keeping their old toys and saving the money if they would prefer.

At the store, teach them to consider what they want and not just go for the first thing that catches their eye. Say, "Let's walk around the whole store once to make sure you don't miss anything and then you can decide." They may need guidance on which toys or clothes will be a better value than others. Ask them to imagine when they will wear the clothes or how many times they think they might play with different toys. This is a great way to teach them to be mindful curators themselves.

Sales and promotions

Sales are an excellent way to save money; however, you're only truly saving money if you're buying something you would have bought anyway. Not all sales are born equal. Some stores hike up their prices one week so they can slash them in a sale the next. Also, putting a mid-range item next to one more expensive can make it look quite reasonable. Price-check everything online before you buy to see what's the best deal for you and if the discounts are as good as the store claims.

Black Friday and deep discounts

Finding a bargain makes us feel particularly excited—just look at the frenzy caused by Black Friday (the only day with its own death count). But Black Friday isn't necessarily the cheapest day to get goods, because some of the "deals" are based on very old prices. The thrill of getting a bargain is dangerous for those trying to practice mindful curation, because it gives us an exaggerated sense of how much we like the product.

A few years ago, I was taken to a staff sale at a designer fashion brand. The original prices of the items were in the thousands of dollars, making the $100 labels in the sale seem as if the shop was giving me free money. I broke my bank account buying several jackets, a dress, and a handbag. It was only a few weeks later, when I was trying to make the jackets fit into my life and my wardrobe, that I realized my mistake. The jackets were never worn and the dress was so badly made it ended up in a costume box despite its original $1,000 price tag.

Instead of reacting to sales, first decide what you want and then bide your time, getting a sense of what the item costs in different places. Then, when it is discounted . . . pounce!

A note on free gifts: Never buy something because it comes with a free gift unless both the product and the free gift are things that you're already committed to buying. (I'm not sure this has ever happened.)

SALESPEOPLE

Have you ever walked into a shop, tried on tons of things, and felt you should buy one of them because the sales staff might think you're a time-waster otherwise? Have you ever bought something because the salesperson seemed so genuine in their belief that it was right for you? I've done both several times. It's only human. All our animal instincts tell us to be nice and cooperate for the good of the tribe. But is this good for *us*? Salespeople can be genuinely warm and caring people that we get on with like an H&M on fire, but that's *not* a good enough reason to buy from them.

You should never feel that you have to buy something to justify your presence in a shop. You are within your rights to see what is available. If an item doesn't please you enough to buy it, then the brand is simply not right for you. So many of us, especially women, are brought up to put their own best interests aside for the sake of pleasing others. Don't let yourself people-please your way into buyer's regret. The salesperson will soon get over their disappointment that you didn't buy whatever it was they were suggesting. But you could be stuck with an object you don't want, a big hole in your bank account, and a little crack in your self-esteem.

INSIDE THE MIND OF A SALESPERSON

I was told by award-winning salesman Theo Davis that the main reasons people buy from a salesperson are:

1. They like the salesperson.

2. They trust the salesperson.

3. They like the product.

In that order.

I suggest that if you like the salesperson, ask them for coffee. Do *not* buy from them unless Number 3 is true. But how do you let them down? Theo says that salespeople can handle being told yes or no. What kills them is the maybes, so say no firmly but nicely.

A well-trained salesperson will be genuinely helpful, but there are some who will do or say almost anything to make the sale. Some will use neurolinguistic programming (NLP), social pressure, or downright lies to "close the deal." There are sales blogs out there that advise salespeople to "push on" even if the customer has said no four times, because they say that 80 percent of sales happen at that point.

Tips for buying from salespeople

I believe that many customers end up buying products just to get themselves out of an awkward situation. Prepare yourself before leaving the house.

- Go in armed with research, a checklist of your personal criteria, and a clear budget.

- Discover if they are a good salesperson. Explain your needs and see if they really listen. Are they answering your questions properly or talking about unrelated features?

- If you're feeling undue pressure (social pressure, emotional blackmail, embarrassment) to buy something and are unsure, remove yourself from the situation immediately and do more research.

- Feel good about saying no firmly and kindly. It means you're not wasting their time.

- If you say no and they persist, walk away. Have a last-resort plan of escape ready, such as needing to talk it through with your partner/friend/guinea pig.

Emotional blackmail

When one of my closest friends got married, she made the mistake of going alone to her dress fitting. With no one there for moral support, the sales assistants pounced on her. "I left almost in tears," she said. "While I was there, the women selling accessories forced me to consider more and more add-ons. They make you feel that if you don't fork out for diamantes to cover your dress or a tiara, it means you obviously don't care about your husband enough to make it special." I was horrified. What should have been a joyful and exciting moment left her anxious, angry, and feeling like a cheapskate despite spending thousands on a wedding dress.

It's not just salespeople who emotionally blackmail us into purchases. Family (especially children) can be highly skilled as well, but buying something out of guilt can leave you with a bitter taste and a lot of resentment. If you don't think a purchase is necessary or wise, don't make it, and try to find more positive ways to bond with the pressuring person or child.

CHARITY RAFFLES AND AUCTIONS

Pushing the guilt button is one of the easiest ways to make a person do something. How many times have you bought a raffle ticket or bid for a prize you have no interest in because "it's for charity"? I remember excitedly buying a raffle ticket at a county fair when I was about seven. I wanted to take home the grand prize (a camera), but ended up winning an ashtray in the shape of a foot! Try to steer clear of bidding on anything apart from what you will really cherish. If you want to contribute, give the money and tell them to keep the tickets or the prize—you'll get a double glow from knowing you're helping and giving someone a greater chance of winning something they want.

If you run charity events yourself, consider making the prizes experiences—meals, time with a skilled person, help in the garden, a cleaner for a few hours, a pool party, a week in a vacation house, audio and e-books, etc. If you run a raffle and you have physical objects donated as prizes, consider putting a jar beside each one and getting people to put their raffle ticket in the jar corresponding with the object they would like. This way people will win only the things they really want, the objects will all go to a good home, and no waste or clutter (or child smokers) will have been created.

VACATION SOUVENIRS AND GIFTS

The vacation buy is a peculiar phenomenon. There's sand between your toes and sun on your skin and you feel a deep need to buy a souvenir, so you do. You cram it into your suitcase, bring it back, look at it in the cold gray light of your home country, and realize that it doesn't fit into your life at all. You aren't even sure you like it. What just happened?

I'm going to call this the "vacay effect." Essentially, your whole vacation acted like a 3-D advertising campaign for that product. You're in a positive frame of mind, you're in a living

Instagram photo, and this rubs off on a product that you might mildly like but has no meaning beyond "I was there."

How to avoid the "vacay effect"

When you're in an exotic location and are tempted by an object, squint everything else out and look at the object itself. Picture where you would put it in your home. What would it be replacing? Would its size, shape, color, and tone fit in with your other things? Is there something in it that speaks to you beyond its being a memento? For example, one vacation buy that I don't regret is an engraved gourd I bought in Peru. It shows the whole messy circle of life, and it sits on my writing desk reminding me how interdependent we all are. It's also a lovely thing to hold.

So, if you see an object that fits into your life and would do a better job than photos in helping you remember this moment, then take it home, treasure it, and make sure it can be seen so it can spark conversations and bring back good times. If you can, ask a guide or friendly local to reassure you that no one was exploited in making it—you don't want to be unwittingly funding child or slave labor.

LITTLE PRESENTS "JUST BECAUSE"

Often we buy little gifts either because we are looking for ways to show our appreciation and affection or we feel we should bring a little something when we come back from our time away or go to visit someone. If you're going to someone's house and you feel that you should take a gift, this can feel like a guilt gift. It's something you feel you *should* do rather than something that comes out of the knowledge that your friend or family member would cherish something specific. Question that "should." Is your presence not enough? Would you think less of *them* if they didn't bring a gift to *your* house?

Sometimes it's nice to show you've been thinking of someone when you've been away from them, though. If this is important to you, bake them a cake or make them something. It doesn't even have to be physical—it could be a funny video or a playlist you think they might enjoy. If you must buy something, buy something local that's edible and that you can share. Something that doesn't leave people thinking, "What are we going to do with this?" as you leave. Don't get into the habit of bringing gifts back from business trips or vacations at all, unless you want to keep up this habit for the rest of your life. Airports and hotel gift shops rarely hold items that we will cherish for long anyway. Also, bringing back memorabilia for people who weren't on the trip isn't always appreciated as much as we might hope. They didn't have the experiences we had, so the objects don't hold any meaning for them.

Basically, give people stories, give people time, give people smiles and hugs, give people love. Everything else is just ribbon.

11

The BuyMeOnce
Buying Guide

or

How to Find the Best Stuff
on the Planet

I am sometimes asked, "Does everything on the BuyMeOnce website last forever?" The longest-lasting brand I've found so far is Solidteknics, a cookware manufacturer whose solid steel and iron pans have a multi-century warranty and will most likely be dug up by archaeologists in half a million years. But we can't hold every product to the same standard; a T-shirt brand simply can't replicate Solidteknics' durability. So what we do is find the best products for durability and sustainability in each product category by comparing competitor brands. We do this by asking six questions. This list now forms the heart of all the research we do at BuyMeOnce.

1. What is the product made from? Is this the most durable material for this product? Does it use a more sustainable material than its competitors in the category?

2. How is the product made? Does the way it is made help increase its durability or reusability?

3. Do the reviews of the product back up the claims of the manufacturer? Does it receive better reviews for durability, quality, and reliability than its competitors?

4. Are we happy with the sustainability and ethics of the manufacturing?

5. Does the manufacturer offer the best aftercare and warranties in the category?

6. Does the product look and feel future-proof, rather than like a fad that will soon become obsolete?

The BuyMeOnce website was built to do all the hard work and research so shoppers don't have to, and the preceding questions have to be answered satisfactorily for a product to win certification from BuyMeOnce. This may be a balancing act. For example, sometimes durability must be sacrificed for usability (or all the BuyMeOnce furniture would be made of stone). Much of our research has gone into this chapter, which is designed to be a practical, handy guide for you to dip into when you're buying something. So, feel free to skim it if you're not looking for anything right now. I'll be mentioning specific brands when I feel it's appropriate, but this is just to give examples of what good quality looks like, not a mandate to rush out and buy that brand.

Also, please take the idea of finding "perfection" off the table. Everything you bring into your life is imperfect, from your lover to your toothbrush, and looking for perfection will just make you miserable. Steve Jobs spent a decade deciding on a sofa and had no furniture in his home at all because he couldn't find any that met his standards of perfection. Don't do a Steve. All you can do is make the best choice you can in the time you've allocated, using the knowledge you have.

If you tend to get in too deep with research, allocate a specific amount of research time. The bigger the purchase, the more research time you should allow, but put a limit on it or you can quickly find yourself spending days agonizing over details. If you're making a big purchase and find yourself overwhelmed by choice, take a step back and write down what the variables are in the order that you care about them, for example: longevity, eco-friendliness, style, size, and price. Find the best products in the top couple of variables and choose between those.

How to choose between style and utility

Products come on a sliding scale of art and utility. A Picasso print on your wall is at one end of that scale, the pipe from your toilet is on the other. Everything else exists in the middle. When practicing mindful curation, you need to keep both art and utility in mind, because both will impact how long you have a product in your life. Here's a rule of thumb: Don't sacrifice strength for beauty when strength and utility really matter for the product to be useful. Get the hammer with the lifetime warranty, not the hammer with the pretty plastic handle. If something is going to spend most of its time in a drawer or cupboard anyway, don't be swayed into buying an inferior product by its appearance.

On the other hand, something that you're going to see regularly (like a water jug) needs to be strong, but it is also important that you like the styling. If you get tired of it in a couple years, it's just as broken as if it had cracked physically. In this case, get the highest quality you can afford with styling you can love for the long term.

Home styling advice

When people buy things for their homes, many don't spend enough time discovering what their tastes are first and have no vision of how everything is going to work together. So, before continuing, do the exercise on page 42 to identify your true style. Anything that makes a "statement" is in danger of dating badly, so make sure any statement piece you have is saying something about *you*, not about current trends. Avoid strongly theming a room (e.g., "Moroccan" or "steam punk") unless you strongly believe this is going to be a life-long passion. Instead, use accent items such as framed posters, a feature ornament, and choice fabrics to celebrate your interests and style inclinations.

BEDROOMS AND LIVING AREAS

Once you have a look that you're happy with, try to steer clear of publications and websites that attempt to persuade you that what you have isn't good enough. Remember, you have chosen the look that makes you feel happy and at home; don't let anyone tell you differently.

Before you look

Measure up your room first. Draw a scale floorplan so you can see how big a piece of furniture would be and how much walking space would be left around it. If money is tight, don't shirk from saving up for the pieces you really want. My room was bare for four months—I slept on the floor and lived out of a suitcase—but it was worth it to save up for my dream bed.

Furniture

Mass-produced, cheap, modern furniture will generally age faster than an antique or a quality handmade piece because it relies on being "on trend" and in pristine condition for its value. Once it starts looking a little less than perfect, its value plummets.

Buying old furniture

Solid, beautifully built antique furniture can be found at auction houses and online on eBay and other reselling sites. Antique bedroom furniture has already proved itself by surviving a couple of world wars and the antics of the baby-boomer generation. The trend toward painted, laminate, and Scandinavian furniture means that this top-notch stuff is going cheap in many countries. The benefits of buying this way is that it's often higher quality than what is mass pro-duced now, nothing new needs to be made, and it keeps an item out of landfill or the incinerator.

Look for solid wood pieces. Veneer, unless just used for decorative flourishes, makes any damage hard to fix. Look at the joints. Traditional dovetail and mortise-and-tenon joints mean pieces are likely to last longer. Look for damage. Some can be easily sanded and resealed and some cannot. If you're handy, or willing to pay for repairs, consider a fixer-upper; you'll get a much better price.

Buying new furniture

Look for solid wood pieces. Solid wood means that a piece can usually be sanded and repaired. Wood is also less energy-consuming than metal. Avoid all plastic furniture unless it's from recycled sources, recyclable, and solid in construction. Make sure any wood used is from sustainably managed forests. You'll find these pieces marked with the Forest Stewardship Council (FSC) symbol. Hard woods (oak, beech, elm, teak, mahogany, alder, eucalyptus, ironwood, etc.), as you may expect, are more hard-wearing than soft woods (pine, cedar, and fir). However, a chunky pine table will last decades if you don't mind the notches and marks that will inevitably pattern the top of it. Look for a decent thickness of wood and watch out for any splits, cracks, or warping.

Some furniture-makers will cut corners by using inferior material inside drawers and places that cannot be seen. If you can, have a look inside a piece or ask the manufacturer about hidden parts. Don't accept a piece held together with nails, staples, and glue. Dowels (pegs), metal brackets, screws, or traditional joints are necessary for a sturdy piece of furniture. Reject furniture that uses toxic volatile organic compounds (VOCs); these can become harmful gases in your home.

Consider furniture that is versatile and multipurpose, such as a box trunk that is also a seat. Think about your lifestyle now and how it might change over the next decade. Pick accordingly.

Sofas

Go shopping with your imagination. Many older pieces can be upcycled to create your dream piece of furniture. If you decide to reupholster, look for hardwearing fabrics with a high "rub count" that will hold up to years of use.

Construction

Feel the springs. Make sure they feel close together—mesh or webbing is no substitute for decent springs. You'll often find that the warranty for the sofa is just on the construction of the frame, so choose wisely.

Stuffing

Choose "highly resilient foam" if you can, as it will keep its shape and plumpness longer than fiber and down. Down needs a huge amount of upkeep and the method of plucking geese and ducks alive is horribly cruel.

Upholstery

One hundred percent fabrics are easier to reuse or recycle than blends, and 100 percent polyester from recycled plastics is one of the eco-friendliest and most durable options. If you want a natural fabric, choose 100 percent linen or cotton with a tight heavyweight weave. Avoid normal silk, which is rather delicate for this use and involves boiling silkworms alive. Can the upholstery be taken off and cleaned? If it can, that's a definite bonus. If not, don't despair. My sofa doesn't have this capability and we get around it by covering the seat with pretty throw blankets, which can be washed if the cat comes in from a muddy day.

High-quality leather is extremely durable and can last for decades. However, there is no such thing as eco-friendly leather. The process of raising and slaughtering animals, followed by hide tanning, is very energy-intensive and can be extremely damaging to the environment. There are a couple of high-end fashion brands investing in a zero-impact leather, so hopefully this will spread to sofa production soon. The good news is that there are many old leather sofas in great condition. If nothing but new leather will do, choose a full-grain leather that has been vegetable dyed, and look after it like it's a newborn baby. Rub cream into it, clean it, and stroke it. Singing is optional. (*See our leathercare tips on page 246.*)

Flooring and curtains

Be especially sure to look for hard-wearing floor coverings in places that are going to see a lot of traffic. Consider a separate rug to protect such areas so that you don't have to replace a whole carpet or sand a wooden floor so regularly. Stone is the most durable flooring and will last for centuries, but it will only be appropriate in some houses. Salvaged hardwood floors or hardwood from responsibly managed forests are good choices, as they can almost always be restored back to their original condition with some sanding and polishing. Vinyl flooring is durable and can be found in both recycled and recyclable varieties. This is best used for small rooms to reduce seams, which is where problems often arise. Tiles can last for years, but beware of putting a tiled floor anywhere where something heavy might be dropped, like the kitchen. Steer clear of engineered wood, as it has only a thin layer of veneer on top and therefore can't be sanded down often, if at all.

Carpets

That "new carpet smell" some people like is actually wafts of chemicals being released, something we might want to avoid in our homes. Go for natural fabrics if possible. Companies such as Tretford make eco-friendly and durable soft carpets with cashmere from goat wool. Carpets made of sisal are also durable and eco-friendly, but not soft underfoot, so are best left for hallways. Other carpet manufacturers, such as Interface and Econyl, have solved the durability versus eco-friendly debate by using recycled plastic materials for their carpeting.

Curtains

Keep curtains and blinds simple and classic, as statement curtains are likely to look dated in a few years. Avoid themed or novelty curtains, because if you choose to change the use of the room, you can end up stuck with Miss Piggy curtains in your home office. Silk is known to rot in the sun, whereas fabrics like brocade, cotton canvas, and linen will last longer. Look for a high thread count, as you would for sheets, and be aware that bright colors tend to fade faster than more neutral tones.

Make sure curtains have an interlining (an extra layer between the lining and curtain material). This can extend the longevity of the curtains and acts as an insulating layer, keeping heat in the house and saving on energy bills.

Cheaply made blinds can quickly break, but there are quality blinds available that have the ability to last a lifetime and are covered by extensive warranties.

Lighting

Lighting can be a real opportunity to have fun and show your personality. The choices for lighting fixtures are endless and lifetime warranties abound in this section, as do upcycled, antique, and recycled options. There is very little wear and tear on light fixtures, so try to get them second-hand and save yourself a fortune. If you're buying new, make sure that any metal is rustproof and the whole thing is cleanable once plugged in. Look at it with an eye to selling it later. If it's the kind of thing that would hold its value on eBay, it can be considered a decent investment.

Turning a found object, your favorite drinks bottle or an old family ornament into a light fixture can help create a space that's truly yours and brings a smile every time you flick the switch. I was in an old Italian restaurant in 2013 and noticed some huge bulbous wine casks. I thought there was something gloriously tactile and fun about them, so I took one home and stuffed it full of twinkle lights. Now it sits in the corner of my living room and gives me an active sense of pleasure whenever I see it. And it was completely free.

LED lighting is naturally longer-lasting, but the number of hours on the box is often misleading. The main cause of bulb failure is a buildup of heat, and only a few manufacturers have actively tried to solve this. The Blume bulb is designed to last a lifetime and is upgradable and recyclable, making it the first truly circular economy light bulb.

Bedding

You spend a third of your life on your mattress. If you knew you were going to spend a third of your life with a stranger, you would probably spend a decent amount of time finding out who they were and checking they didn't make you feel uncomfortable or have a habit of ruining your sex life. Get promiscuous and try out as many mattresses as you can. (If you have particular back issues, ask your doctor or physical therapist for advice before you go.) Warranties abound, but your best bet is to choose the highest-quality materials. Natural latex is the most durable mattress material you can find, and SleepingOrganic offers an organic latex mattress with a twenty-year warranty, so you don't need to worry about your bed being toxic.

Many mattress companies will try to persuade you that you need to replace your mattress every eight years for hygiene and comfort reasons. While it is true that dust, dust mites, and sweat can accumulate in your mattress, a decent waterproof mattress-protector will prevent much of the buildup. You can also vacuum your mattress periodically or take it outside and beat it, and flipping it over and turning it head to tail every three months will keep it comfortable. If you don't see any sagging or deterioration of the mattress and it feels fine after eight years, there's no reason not to keep going and going.

Pillows and bedding

Choose organic latex pillows. They're cruelty-free, hypoallergenic, help prevent dust mites, and are the most durable option available. Organic Textiles makes a few options.

You can also find high-quality bamboo sheets with a lifetime guarantee from Cariloha. Bamboo is my optimum choice, as it generally requires much less water and fewer chemicals to produce than cotton. The next best thing would be one hundred percent Egyptian cotton sheets at the highest thread count you can afford. Beware of "Egyptian-quality" cotton sheets. This is a marketing ploy and is the equivalent of "chicken-flavored" instant noodles (which are, bizarrely, vegetarian).

HOME OFFICE

Many office accessories are just various ways of dealing with paper, so try as much as possible to become a zero-waste and paper-free office. Also, it is inadvisable to spend many hours in one position, and my edict to choose solid wood furniture doesn't work when it comes to the office chairs.

Office chairs

I started writing this book on my sturdy, solid wooden kitchen chair, but, before long, all the sitting took its toll on my back. There's no point sacrificing your spine for the solid-wood cause. Apart from anything else, your spine is considerably more expensive to replace. Consider a kneeling or ergonomic chair (one that has been designed to support your back properly). Many of these are made predominantly from plastic, but you can find plastic chairs that are "cradle-to-cradle" certified. This means the manufacturer has thought about the materials they've put into it and designed it to be recyclable. Herman Miller is one of the best brands I've found in this category and they have one of the longest warranties.

Sitting for long periods of time is damaging, so consider getting a sit-stand desk or a simple box that raises the level of your computer. Standing while working takes some getting used to, but it keeps you more alert, burns calories, strengthens your legs and core, and could make your butt look cuter in shorts.

Desk lamp

Lamps are more likely to be thrown out for style or convenience reasons than for breakages, so be sure a lamp is right for you before you buy. Can you adjust it? Is it the right height? Does it give off enough light? Is the cord long enough? Would you be happy to look at it for several decades? Might it work in another room if you ever have to rearrange your space?

You can find many beautiful lamps made from eco-friendly materials, such as bamboo or driftwood. If you go for ceramic or glass, make sure the lamp isn't placed somewhere it can be knocked over. After that, it's just a question of putting a bulb into it that you won't need to replace. Blume, mentioned on page 174, is one such bulb and has just come onto the market.

Desk

See pages 169–171.

Stationery, accessories, and storage

Keeping your data digitally means it is easily searchable and less physical storage is needed—just be sure to back it up both on an external drive and in the cloud to be extra safe. If you do have to deal with lots of paper, avoid plastic solutions and use a staple-free stapler or water-activated gummed paper tape. Anything paper you need to buy, such as notebooks or binders, can be both recycled and recyclable. Store important documents and paperwork in a flexible and easy-to-navigate system, such as hanging files, to prevent a jumble of box-files and binders.

Also, if you choose to invest in a pen like mine, the Fisher Space Pen Infinium, which has enough ink to last the average person a lifetime, you can say good-bye to all those cheap plastic pens that seem to breed in jars in your kitchen.

KITCHEN

Kitchenware is one of the few categories where there is still a reasonable number of long-lasting products. Items that can probably last your lifetime (if you take care of them) include knives, cutting boards, pots and pans, bakeware, coffee grinders and pepper/salt mills, and wooden, steel, or silicone utensils and cutlery. Kitchen things that will probably break include glassware, dinnerware, small electrical appliances, gadgets, and baking scales.

Knives

Physically test a few different knives if you can, as we all have different needs, depending on how often we cook and what kind of cooking we do. If you have small hands, you'll get on better with shorter knives and vice versa for bigger hands. A good knife will be "full tang," meaning that the blade extends into the handle, and should balance well in your hand. To test this, place your finger between the blade and the handle and see if the knife will rest there.

Some of the best brands we've found are Wüsthof and Global, and we prefer wood or metal to plastic handles. I'd recommend a universal knife block so if you buy knives from different brands they will still fit. A good set of knives can last a lifetime if cared for. (*See page 259 for knife care.*)

Cutting boards

To help with knife care, be sure to use a cutting board. A chunky wooden or bamboo board is best, and boards that have been glued together to look like chunky chessboards have self-healing properties, as the grain knits back together when it's sliced. (*See page 260 for cutting-board care.*)

Pots and pans

Cast iron or carbon steel make the best skillets and frying pans, and will last the longest, especially if, like Solidteknics pans, they are made of a single piece of steel with no rivets to loosen and cause handle wobbles. You can also find several excellent lifetime-guaranteed pan brands in both copper and stainless steel. These are very similar materials in strength and durability, but copper conducts heat better (often ideal for chefs) and stainless steel is generally lighter in weight.

Classic enameled cast-iron pots made by brands such as Le Creuset should also last decades if you don't burn food on the bottom or scratch the enamel with metal implements or scrubbers. The toughest nonstick is made by Le Creuset and is lifetime warrantied. However, there are increasing calls for people to steer clear of nonstick surfaces and use natural seasoning due to worries about chemicals leaching into food. See page 257 for how to season your pan, which is a more natural and sustainable way of achieving a nonstick surface.

Bakeware

Avoid nonstick surfaces with bakeware, as they can scratch and lower the life expectancy of the pan. Look for materials such as anodized aluminum, which are resistant to rust and blistering. There are also versatile pans available, such as those made by Alan Silverwood, where you can adjust the shape of the baking area, meaning you don't have to buy lots of different sizes.

Coffee grinders and pepper/salt mills

Look for grinder mechanisms made of ceramic or case-hardened stainless steel to keep them sharp and protect them from erosion. Ceramic is the toughest and most durable mechanism, and it won't rust. Look for a ceramic conical-burr coffee grinder if you want to keep on grinding into old age. You'll find several manufacturers who guarantee the grinding mechanism. Once you've taken all this into consideration, choose a color finish, shape, and style that won't look dated on your table in ten years' time.

Wooden, steel, or silicone utensils

My first preference would be for well-carved wooden or bamboo utensils from sustainable sources. These are a beautiful and lifelong addition to any kitchen and are sold by countless companies. They are also compostable if they ever do break. Any stainless-steel utensils should be of the highest-quality 18/10 steel; dry them quickly after washing them, and you shouldn't have any rust problems.

Flatware

Look for 18/10 stainless steel with the longest warranty you can find. Liberty Tabletop is one such brand and one of the last still making flatware in the United States. Make sure to pick a style as durable as the set itself. Keep them rust-free by handwashing or take them out of the dishwasher immediately.

Glassware

A good rule of thumb is to see what hotels are using. Hotel glassware is put through rigorous use, so you know it'll stand up to the trials of home use. We recommend glassware made out of High Tech crystal glass (such as the Luigi Bormioli line that offers a twenty-five-year guarantee against chipping), which is significantly more smash-proof than normal glass and has an impressive eco-profile too.

Dinnerware

Your best bet for the longest-lasting plates, cups, and bowls is probably stoneware crockery, made by such brands as Denby, or vitrelle glass crockery, made by Corelle, which are more durable than porcelain.

Small electrical appliances

Appliances are supposed to make your life easier, so do your homework and know what you want to get out of your purchase before heading to the store.

Toaster

Toasters don't tend to have very long warranties, but some are more easily repaired than others. Find a toaster, such as a Dualit, that can be taken apart and repaired, and avoid over-complicated models with too many unnecessary functions.

Mixer

Mixers are one of the few appliances that do seem to stand the test of time. The Ankarsrum Original beat the competition for the most durable mixer, although there are plenty of good brands in this category. This model has several different functions, which saves on buying separate equipment such as spiralizers, meat grinders, and pasta makers. Only get one if you're a regular chef, though, because an occasional cake can easily be mixed by hand, saving you several hundred dollars and toning your arms at the same time.

Blender

If you blend a lot (for example, make a smoothie every day), invest in an industrial blender and you can be blending for years to come. We've identified Blendtec and Vitamix as the best brands.

Gadgets

Avoid specialized gadgets if you can. Many items, such as egg separators and spiralizers, just aren't necessary, and cheap plastic implements serve the gift market far better than the people who receive them. Pizza scissors and novelties that turn your fried eggs into penis shapes? Just say no.

The only gadget you might need if you're a keen cook is a mortar and pestle. Get a chunky one and it should last forever.

Baking scales

Mechanical scales are likely to last longer than digital ones and come with the bonus of not requiring batteries. Choose a sturdy set with a metal bowl, such as Salter's Sweetie Mechanical Kitchen Scale, which comes with a fifteen-year guarantee.

Kitchenware to avoid

We can cut down dramatically on our household waste with a few simple swaps, such as using reusable food wrap (there are some made with beeswax cloths or silicone) instead of plastic wrap. Also, be aware of hidden chemicals in cheap storage containers or serveware. Avoid, where you can:

- Anything plastic (if you must buy plastic, make sure it's BPA-free).

- Melamine in kids' dishware and glasses. It can be mixed with natural materials (such as bamboo) and breaks down when heated, releasing chemicals into the food.

- Anything cheap and flimsy, "just for now," or disposable.

Other "zero-waste" swaps you can make:

- Cloths instead of paper towels. You can find washable bamboo cloths on a roll.

- Reusable silicone bags instead of zip-top bags.

- Cloth, canvas, or mesh bags for shopping.

- Reusable metal or silicone straws instead of disposable ones.

- Reusable plastic or metal storage containers rather than one-use foil, paper, or plastic boxes.

- A flask, canteen, or travel mug rather than plastic or paper cups.

- A titanium spork instead of plastic cutlery on the go.

TOOLS

I recently found out that the average electric drill gets used for only twenty minutes in its entire life.[1] Buy as few tools as possible; there's almost always a neighbor or family member you can borrow from. An adjustable screwdriver set, an adjustable wrench, a set of Allen keys, and a hammer are more than enough to deal with average household tasks. Buy a high-quality stainless-steel set with a lifetime warranty (available from a few different brands such as Snap-On and Craftsman).

SPORTS, HOBBIES, AND LEISURE

Rent before you buy if you can, and make sure that you're really going to pursue the hobby before you invest in an expensive set-up. BuyMeOnce has only just scratched the surface when it comes to sports and hobby equipment. I'm particularly fond of Manduka's lifetime-guaranteed yoga mats and the invincible One World Futbol, but with everything from base-jumping parachutes to pottery wheels to research, it's going to take us a while to get a comprehensive list.

This is where the experts come in. If you're looking for equipment, call up clubs, societies, and groups or post on their forums and Facebook pages asking for advice. You'll get much more independent advice from enthusiasts than from retailers. Tell them you're specifically looking for longevity in what you want to buy.

TECHNOLOGY AND APPLIANCES

We are used to bigger, better, and more bewitching tech coming out every year. We've been trained to expect the new, demand the new, and, if we're willing to pay for it, get the new. But the key to buying tech is to sort the real technological advances from the superficial ones, and these might not be the same for every person. For some buyers, a phone with a better camera might be a game-changer for their business, but for many of us it might just mean we can see every pixel of our freckles when we take a selfie.

If your current technology is doing everything you need it to do, there's no reason at all to replace it with the latest model. We need to start demanding our tech is upgraded, not replaced. This is possible, and a couple of forward-thinking technology companies have adopted modular options as part of their conscientious policy, such as Fairphone, which we have identified as the BuyMeOnce smartphone company of choice.

Smartphones

The Fairphone is the BuyMeOnce mobile phone because it is designed to be upgraded and fixed. Each part can be replaced and customized. Want a better camera? No problem. Need more storage? You've got it. On top of that, Fairphone offers double the usual warranty and stands out for using ethically sourced raw materials for phones.

If you're wedded to the brand you currently use, get as much space as possible when you buy a new phone, as this may well determine how long it lasts, and be prepared to get the battery replaced at some point. Then get the best case you can find, such as the Mous Limitless case. If you have repeatedly dropped your phone in the sink, bath, or toilet, as I have, you might want to invest in a waterproof case.

Laptops

Most people agree that Apple currently makes the most reliable and durable laptops, but if you buy a PC laptop, go for one that's easy to upgrade and fix. This usually means a slightly chunkier model. Lenovo's ThinkPad for Professionals is one of the best. This is a fast-moving world, though, so look to the forums, retailers, and, of course, the BuyMeOnce site for which brands are currently doing the best in this regard.

Desktop computers

If you're buying a PC desktop, consider buying a PC tower, as it is more modular and has better longevity than laptops or all-in-one versions. One of these can easily last over ten years. Asus is one of the most reliable brands in this category. Apple desktops also have high reliability ratings, but are more likely to become obsolete because they cannot be upgraded.

Printers

Printer companies make their money by selling expensive cartridges and cheap printers that break frequently. (Some of these ink cartridges even say they are empty when they are not, so we throw them away sooner.) The best we've found is the Epson EcoTank. It comes with two years' worth of ink, and takes affordable refill bottles. A three-year warranty is also about as good as you get in the printing game. We like this because it also reduces the need for wasteful ink cartridges.

TV

We currently replace our TVs roughly every eight years, but if we pick well there's no reason why a TV shouldn't last us a couple of decades. Panasonic is currently rated the most reliable TV brand. Companies are constantly trying to enhance the picture quality of TVs to tempt us into a new purchase, but there are some picture enhancements that you may not feel are necessary, such as curved screens or 4K.

Smart home systems

I worry that these devices allow brands to get inside your home and talk to you in an unprecedented way. As I write, Campbell's is giving out recipes on Amazon Echo and other companies are queuing up to make apps or "skills" for this bit of tech so that they can gain access to our lives. We do not yet know where this could lead.

These systems are also another thing to fix and upgrade and make your life more complicated. Amazon Echo seems to trump Google for functionality, but still don't do it. You can turn your own lights off.

Headphones

The current BuyMeOnce favorite is Sennheiser HD-25. These headphones were originally designed for audio engineers and are revered by DJs for their excellent sound quality. We at BuyMeOnce like them because they are completely modular, so you can repair or replace broken parts. They come with a two-year warranty, but many users have them for over a decade.

We also have high hopes for business models such as Gerrard Street, who rent you high-quality headphones and take responsibility for any repairs if they are needed. They are only in Holland at the moment, but we're hoping this model might spread.

APPLIANCES

I am fighting to make it easier for people to make good choices on appliances by putting the expected lifespan on the packaging of every item (rather like the energy efficiency label). You can help by signing the #makeitlast petition. But until I win this fight, appliances are hard to judge as a shopper, and we have to rely on independent testers and reviews.

Washing machines and dishwashers

For all large appliances, be mindful of the energy rating and try to go for more efficient models; most good modern appliances are now up in the A++ ratings. Unfortunately, we know that washing machine durability has been going down over the years. The most we can hope for now is a ten-year warranty. The best brands for durability are Miele or Speed Queen. Both keep it simple, so there are fewer features than on some ultra-modern machines, but that can mean less to go wrong too.

Avoid top-loaders, as they are more wasteful, and make sure that the drum isn't sealed in, or you'll find yourself having to replace the whole machine for what should be a simple repair. This year we got the exciting news that a modular washing machine is in development and will have a fifty-year guarantee. This groundbreaking machine will be called L'increvable. Be sure to check BuyMeOnce.com for updates.

Refrigerators and freezers

Many people now like to tuck their fridge away behind cabinetry, but having a freestanding fridge/freezer gives you more choice of brands and allows you to move it or take it with you if you move. Go frost-free to prevent food waste and cut down on fridge maintenance; apart from that, the fewer complications and gadgets, like water dispensers, the less there is to go wrong. Bosch comes out as the best overall brand, with excellent reliability, and Samsung is the brand that stays fault-free for the longest.[2]

Vacuum cleaners

Choose a cleaner that matches your living situation; for example, if you have lots of stairs, get a cleaner that's easy to carry. If you have pets, make sure the model picks up pet hair well. As of 2017, Henry, Miele, and Bosch make the longest-lasting vacuum cleaners.[3]

SEASONAL DECOR

Americans spend a spooky two billion dollars on Halloween decorations each year, most of which are thrown away.[4] Increasingly, there's a lot of pressure to go big on Christmas and Halloween. We pay for it once and then the environment pays the price again. Don't get into competition with your neighbors to see who has the most flashing reindeer. Let them win.

That's not to say we should go full Grinch and have no decorations. I recommend having one or two reusable high-impact pieces that can become a family tradition. My mother always decorates the house by pinning Christmas cards along stretches of red ribbon, which she's been reusing for decades. In my own home, we have a BuyMeOnce tree, which we've kept alive by planting in a large pot in the garden. It's small, but has enormous character; we call it Bob. Other sustainable tree options are to rent a tree that is replanted or to buy an eco-friendly fake tree. Build up a collection of decorations slowly by only buying memorable pieces that spark happy memories or mean something to your family.

Try to make other decorations as eco-friendly as possible. Buy things you're going to reuse, or natural items such as real pumpkins for Halloween (which can then be made into soup) or sprigs of holly cut from the garden for Christmas.

PRODUCTS TO AVOID FOR A SIMPLER LIFE

At its heart, mindful curation seeks a balance between meaning and simplicity. Most of us look at our lives and crave more simplicity. What is both hilarious and terrifying is that marketing people have realized this and are offering a range of items to "simplify our lives"—everything from glasses that help us watch TV lying down to watermelon slicers and 2-in-1 items like "a garden trowel that is also a bottle opener." I'm afraid that the only way to really simplify your life is to realize you don't need so much stuff, turn that realization into action and declutter, then only bring into your life stuff that you need, does its job well, and won't need to be replaced regularly.

Specialist items

Generally, specialist items like watermelon slicers are just extra clutter. How much watermelon do you have to eat to justify buying a watermelon slicer? More than is good for your digestive system certainly. Often there is a classic object, like an excellent knife, that can do the job just as well.

Gimmicky gadgets

The idea of being able to watch TV while lying down might be appealing and quite amusing, but would you be willing to wear a pair of glasses to do it? In almost every case, these glasses will be worn once or twice for a laugh and then languish in a drawer with a mix of other "not sure what to do with this" stuff.

"Smart home" gadgets

The "internet of things" is moving swiftly into our homes and promising to make life easier for us by switching off our lights and letting our appliances talk to one another. Before being tempted into technology such as this, bear in mind that it can add extra complications. If it needs servicing, upgrading, fixing, and replacing regularly, like most new tech does, it may be more trouble than it's worth. How stressful is turning lights on and off anyway? Smart appliances may also be hackable, and home hub systems are already being used to advertise to us. Unless you want your fridge to start giving you dinner suggestions from companies who have paid to invade your home, I would steer clear of bringing this sort of tech into your life.

CLOTHES

When I choose clothing, I often make the material my priority. The quality and feel of the material we choose to put next to our skin can have a surprising impact on our mood and behavior.

Materials

Slipping your body into a beautifully soft, natural fabric is a way to nurture yourself and the planet at the same time. All clothing production has an environmental impact, but some manufacturers make significantly more effort than others to make their clothes as kind to you and our planet as possible. (*Go to tarabutton.com/materials for a list of materials and their qualities.*)

Construction

Sometimes it can be difficult to assess a garment's quality. This is when an eye for build-quality and craftsmanship will come in handy. Look for items with "self-facings," i.e., the fabric of the cuffs and collars should be the same on both the outside and the inside. Are the seams and stitching tight and compact, not loose and perhaps about to unravel? Double rows of stitching and French seams (where the raw edges of the fabric are neatly tucked away and sewn down on the inside of the garment) are a sign that that piece has been made to last.

Prints and patterns should align and meet neatly across seams unless intentionally avoided due to design. If there is a lining, it should be properly placed in the garment to allow for movement. If you're unsure about a garment's lining, gently pull at it and see how easily it begins to separate from the garment's body. A lack of lining isn't always a sign of poor quality; sometimes the construction of a garment is so perfect and beautiful that designers want to show off their work.

If you fall for something and it isn't well made, try to resist it. If you can't resist, be prepared to ask a tailor to reinforce it for you. You should be able to walk around, sit, and stretch without what you're wearing becoming a bunched-up mess. Make sure you take a few turns around the dressing room, squat, and lunge (yes LUNGE!) to road test the garment before you commit.

Fit

If the garment is too small for you, don't buy it hoping you'll fit into it one day. If an item is slightly too big but perfect in every other way, consider getting it tailored to fit. Certain alterations are easier to do than others. Hems and cuffs are easy, as are adding darts to give a shirt or pair of trousers more shape. If the seams around the shoulders need altering, that is a trickier proposition. If in doubt, locate a tailor and call them for advice before you purchase.

SHOES

When shopping for shoes, focus on their purpose, look for the highest-quality materials, and buy from companies that will help you if you have any issues with the shoes in the future. Most of all, go for versatility.

My wedding gave me an opportunity to buy a pair of really special shoes, but the pair I chose, while stunningly beautiful, are also comfortable and will go with everything from my wedding dress to a nice pair of jeans, so I'll be able to wear them long into the future.

Construction

Any stitching needs to be impeccable, with no gaps. And you shouldn't be able to see any glue. Leather is the most durable material, but be sure to ask for full-grain. This is the highest-quality and longest-lasting leather. If it's not full grain, it will begin to look plastic over time. There are also vegan leather options available. Consider pineapple leather, which is new on the scene but eco-friendlier than the standard pleather that's made out of petrochemicals.

For men's (and for some traditional women's) shoes, ask for a Goodyear welt, which refers to the way the upper is attached to the sole. This is the traditional, most work-intensive, durable, and fixable of all shoe constructions.

Shape

Don't go for extreme shapes in shoes, as they will date very quickly. Avoid plastic soles, as that is a sign of inferior quality; rubber or leather is a better option. Run your finger inside the shoe and check that the lining doesn't bubble and has enough padding to cushion your foot.

Fit

Make sure you walk around enough in the shoes to get a good idea of how your foot and the shoe get on. Any pinching and it won't be a good marriage. (*See page 248 for shoe care and storage tips.*)

ACCESSORIES

The most important thing when it comes to accessories is that the style is chosen in accordance with your true taste, as opposed to what's in fashion. Once you've decided what type of accessory you think you'd like to wear long term, you can start looking for the best-quality example. For any leather accessories, follow the same rules as laid out in the following "Bags" section. For bags, purses, and wallets, darker colors are a safer bet as they don't show dirt nearly as much. You can find jewelry that is ethical, uses recycled metals, and comes with a lifetime guarantee. In particular, always be aware of where diamonds come from, and go for vintage or ethically sourced stones. Having your jewelry custom designed will ensure that it remains relevant to you in the long term.

Multifunctional accessories can also be a good investment. A Turkish peshtemal has multiple uses, from a scarf to a blanket, and Luks Linen offers peshtemals with a twenty-year guarantee. And look for a super-durable umbrella; we at BuyMeOnce like Davek for their lifetime warranty. Some umbrellas even have a chip in them to tell you if you've left them behind. If you do lose them, you get 50 percent off a replacement.

Classic knitted accessories can last a long time if made with the best-quality wool. Myssyfarmi guarantees their hats for life. As does Tilley, who makes classic cotton summer toppers. Hair accessories are often flimsy and easily lost. If you put your hair up a lot, look for a substantial hair grip that is harder to lose, like a chopstick, a leather barrette with a wooden pin, or a metal clasp. For plain hair ties, Burlybands are pretty chunky and last longer than average.

Bags

A handbag or a satchel is a particularly important investment piece. No item in your wardrobe will go through more than the bag you use every day or the luggage you travel with. Look for a well-lined bag with reinforced stitching. Leather, nylon, and canvas are the most durable materials, but vegan leather is also available. If you want to tell if the bag you've just fallen for is a high-quality, well-made item, open it up immediately and look inside. Poorly made bags, even expensive ones, will often have zero attention to detail on the internals. Here are some other clues as to whether a bag will last:

- A high-quality bag will have fully finished and usually hand-painted edges. Raw or exposed edges aren't a good sign—these will likely tear or fray.

- A durable lining is essential. Look for grosgrain, jacquard, or twill weaves; these will stand you in good stead.

- Hardware (including zippers and zip pulls) should have proper metal content and be properly fixed to the bag.

- Durability feet on bags and luggage are highly useful, as even the slightest elevation will protect the bag from wear on the bottom. Feet can also be easily replaced, whereas leather on the base panel of a bag cannot.

- Handles are a real telltale sign of impeccable or shoddy craftsmanship. Try them out too, if you can. If they don't sit comfortably, your investment will be wasted.

EXTRA ADORNMENTS/GROOMING PRODUCTS

A grooming product might claim to help you achieve a "hassle free" look, but anything that means adding an extra layer of fuss to your day should be weighed carefully. It's easy for makeup, hair, nail art, jewelry, and styling to become a burden rather than a joy. A 2016 study of 2,000 people found that the longer they spent getting ready, the more likely they were to feel negative about their appearance.[5] And some people can take up to two hours to get ready in the morning.[6] That could mean spending *two whole years* of your life getting ready. Think of all the fun you could have in that time!

Makeup

Experiment with getting your makeup collection down to a capsule collection. I have my famous five—concealer, mascara, eye shadow, blush, and lip balm are all I wear. Look for organic and ethically made brands that offer refills, as these are better both for your skin and the planet. I take off my makeup using round, bamboo fabric pads, which I can then chuck in the washing machine, saving on disposable wipes. You can find sturdy wooden makeup brushes from brands such as Ecotools. We also like Tweezerman tweezers, as they offer free sharpening for life.

Toothbrush

Consider a zero-waste toothbrush unless you're an electric toothbrush person; in which case, scour the reviews for reliability and battery life in particular.

Razor

Huge amounts of waste are produced by disposable razor blades. We recommend getting a safety razor, which is very easy to use, or, if you're up for a challenge, a straight razor that you sharpen with a leather strop.

Hairbrush

Hairbrushes can hold up very well if they're not too cheap. Go for natural wood and bristles to reduce their environmental impact.

BUYING FOR BABIES

The arrival of a new baby is a time when all our nesting instincts are running riot. It's a joyful but anxious time, and every marketer of baby products knows this. They may not mean to do it, but there is a lot of "fear selling." If you're feeling anxious, look around at all the adults in the world. We managed to survive infancy without wipe warmers, steam sterilizers, and "pee pee teepees" (look them up if you dare).

With that in mind, other than the warmth and love that you will give the child, here is a list of the essentials a baby needs.

Baby clothes

   5 to 7 sleepsuits
   5 to 7 sleeveless or short-sleeved bodysuits or vests
   5 to 7 long-sleeved bodysuits

3 pairs of socks
3 pairs of booties
2 or 3 hats
2 or 3 cardigans

(When you buy these, think about what the temperature will be when your child will use them.)

Nursery furniture

1 Moses basket, crib, or cot
1 mattress (buy new)
1 baby monitor, if needed
1 changing mat (or you can have just one portable one)

Linen

6 muslin squares/wraps for burping
2 to 4 bottom sheets
2 to 4 top sheets and 2 or 3 blankets *or* 1 or 2 baby sleeping bags

Out and about

1 hooded waterproof jacket for yourself (it's harder to hold an umbrella while pushing a stroller)
1 carrier suitable from birth
1 bag big enough for diapers, bottles, etc.
1 portable changing mat
1 car seat that adjusts from birth to two years

Diaper-changing

Diapers, newborn size, either biodegradable or reusable
Biodegradable diaper bags
Wipes (reusable or biodegradable)

Breastfeeding

3 nursing bras
Breast pads

Bottlefeeding

6 feeding bottles
6 nipples, slow flow
1 sterilizer
Infant formula, if you're not breastfeeding; breast
    pump, if you are breastfeeding

When decorating a baby's room, I believe there's no need to buy decor that screams, "Baby!" Remember that every other item in the room—the cuddly toys, clothes, bedding, books, and the *baby*—will be screaming "Baby!" For the "backdrop," such as walls, curtains, carpet, lights, and wardrobe, choose decor that your child will still be comfortable with at ten years old, or fifteen, twenty, even thirty-five. They will likely be coming back all their life.

Consider getting a few large picture frames for the wall. The pictures within them can be updated from fairy tales to superheroes to favorite music groups as the child grows and their interests and tastes change. If there's space, add an attractive cork or magnetic board to attach meaningful letters and photos to. This, together with the picture frames, allows your kids to express their individuality without wholesale redecoration.

If you choose to invest in a piece of children's furniture, consider getting something that can adapt as your child grows. The Tripp Trapp chair is an example of modular brilliance—it can be used from birth and adjusted gradually, allowing your child to use it right up to sitting in a proper chair.

Outside the baby's room, a stroller is often one of the biggest purchases. Think about what it needs to do to fit into your life—does it need to fold quickly or survive muddy walks? The best brand that we've found for design and durability is Stokke.

Go organic and natural with fabrics and clothing, especially for young babies, as their skin is so sensitive. Also, buy as big as you can (without your child becoming uncomfortable), so that you can ensure the greatest amount of wear out of the clothing. There are some adjustable kids' clothing brands out there, such as Nula, which can increase the lifespan of clothes dramatically.

I think there's an impulse to buy new things for a baby, but because infancy is such a short time, there are millions of families with unused stuff cluttering their homes. Before you buy, you'll probably be surprised at how much you can borrow or be given. My sister Juliet took full advantage of this for her new little one and was pretty much given everything she needed after posting that she was looking for baby things online and on her community noticeboard.

Buying toys

The BuyMeOnce toy brands are a lovely combination of both sustainable and durable—toxin-free wooden toys and hardy recycled plastic ones. They should be tough enough to be passed down to many children, and some are beautiful enough to become heirlooms. Blocks are particularly good, as they can be used again and again in different ways. However, toys can be a bit of a minefield. We know that only three months after Christmas, half of kids' toys will be broken. And the number of toys we buy our children is rather staggering. In the West, six out of ten parents admit that they get their kids the latest clothes and collectable toys as soon as they ask for them.[7] Only about 3 percent of the world's children live in America, but they own 40 percent of the toys consumed globally.[8]

A balanced approach is needed here. We shouldn't dismiss the material things that our kids obsess over as trivial and wasteful but rather wait to figure out what is a fad and what is a genuine interest. Kids often say they want the same thing as their friends when their friends are showing off toys, but if given a bit of time and space and left to choose with their own interests and passions, they might choose something different. Kids can, in fact, have so many toys that they never learn to focus on one thing, and it can also prevent them from using their imagination. A nursery in Germany took away all the children's toys for three months and found that while the children were initially bewildered, the boredom forced them to make up their own games and, before long, they realized they could have just as much fun without toys. They also socialized and concentrated better.[9]

You must decide what is right for your family, but keeping toy buying to an occasional treat and having a "one-in one-out" system can slow the cycle of perpetual consumption and help your kids value the things they have. A toy library is a particularly good way of adding novelty into your child's play without having to own the toy. If one toy is a particular hit, you can consider getting your child a version of their own.

12

Keeping and Caring

or

How to Hold on to the
Things You Love

The "make do and mend" culture we've had throughout most of history died with the mass production of cheap goods, making it easier to throw away and replace than to care and repair. When we practice mindful curation, however, the products we bring into our life will be high-quality, meaningful, and worthy of maintenance and mending, which is why we need to rediscover this lost art. This chapter helps you to make decisions on when to repair and when to replace and crucially how not to lose the things you love. For a practical and detailed guide on how to get some of your favorite things to last as long as possible and for a full list of the yearly maintenance tasks we should all do around the home, go to Appendix I.

WHEN SOMETHING BREAKS

Get to know your local tailor, shoe repairer, carpenter, and handyman. Ask them if they can give you tips on how to mend simple things yourself and how to make products last longer.

Find your Mr. Fixit

Outdoor clothing company Patagonia says that "repair is a radical act," and it is! Certainly, it now goes against what most companies want us to do. Repair is one of our best defenses against planned obsolescence, and whole communities have sprung up around the idea of mending something rather than replacing it, so find the handy person in your local community. It might be someone you have to pay or it might be a friend and family member. Ask their advice before buying a product, and find out which ones are fixable and have spare parts available.

Repair or replace?

When you look at a faulty item, usually vague mental gymnastics take place: "How much would it cost to fix? How long would it last even if I did fix it? And how much would a new one cost?" Those are the practical questions, but there are often emotional ones too: "Do I love this item? Does it have any meaning over and above what it does for me? Do I like the look of it? Does that even matter? Are the new models a significant improvement?" Let's cut through the mental clutter. I've broken the "repair or replace" decision-making down into three main questions.

1. Would I Use and Keep It If It Still Worked?

If yes, find out how much it would be to get it fixed. If it's less than 50 percent of a new BuyMeOnce version of the item, get it fixed.

If no:

- Get it fixed and try to sell it.

- Donate it to a charity that will fix it.

- Sell it for someone else to fix.

- Send it back to the manufacturer, telling them you trust they will find out what is wrong with it and make their future products better.

- Recycle it.

2. Can It Be Restored to Full Working Condition?

If yes, this is by far the eco-friendliest thing to do, unless the product is a very old electrical item that uses significantly more power than a new one would.

If no, can it be upcycled or reused in a different way? If no to those, recycle it.

3. If It Can't Be Repaired, Am I Emotionally Attached to It?

If yes, is there a way of displaying it or upcycling it into a product that adds value to your life?

If no, can it be upcycled or reused in a different way? If no to those, recycle it.

HOW NOT TO LOSE THINGS

I used to be the mistress of losing things, but a life less throwaway has been very useful in this regard. It has been estimated that we will spend around 150 days of our lives searching for lost items.[1] That's ten decent two-week vacations we're missing out on. Save this time by following these tips.

Everything in its place

Always knowing where something will be creates an immediate sense of calm for me. This not only prevents losing possessions, it also guards against that groaning lazy feeling when you know you have a chore to do but you don't know where the relevant stuff is. If I know where the vacuum is lurking, the stairs are much more likely to become cat-hair free.

Once you've gone through the taking stock exercise (see page 124), give everything in your home a place of its own. Store items close to the area where they are most used. Be as specific as possible. "Stationery goes in this drawer" isn't good enough. Divide up drawers and shelves and pick a place for each object or a cluster of similar objects. Labeling the space is useful both for people putting things away and immediately being able to see if something is missing.

LOSING THINGS OUTSIDE OF THE HOUSE

Most people lose things not in the home but when they move from one place to another—for example, from a car to a restaurant. In fact, taxis, cars, and buses are the most common places for us to lose items. This happens because we don't remember to check as we leave. To fix this situation, try the following exercise.

Dropping things

The second most common reason for losing something is things simply fall out of pockets and bags. Don't overstuff either of these, and have set pockets and slots for things to reduce the need for rummaging. Always zip them if possible. If you have an issue with dropping gloves (which annoyingly make no sound when they fall), clip them to the cuffs of your coat.

PREVENTING LOST PROPERTY

To avoid leaving things behind, we need to set up a habit that will trigger us to check our belongings. Here's where we can steal an advertising tactic and use a catchy jingle to force our brain to remember something.

- Cite the phrase "Stepping out? Turn about!" Set these words to your own tune and sing it to yourself ten times or more.

- At the same time, imagine leaving several different vehicles you travel in regularly. See the car/cab/bus/train clearly in your head in as much detail as possible. Imagine getting out of your seat, saying or singing the jingle in your head, and then turning and looking at where you were sitting to check for anything left behind.

- Do the same when imagining different doors leading outside—restaurant doors, office doors, glass doors, rotating doors, metal doors, wooden doors. The more vivid you can make these images, the better this will work. Imagine walking out alone and with friends or family distracting you. Either way, say/sing the jingle and turn around to check.

- The next time that you're in a transitional situation, you know what to do. Eventually it will become a habit and you will turn around and check naturally with no effort whatsoever.

- If you have kids, teach them the jingle too. Sing it with them when you leave your seats on the bus or get out of a car, until it's stuck in their heads. It will be a great tool for them in the future.

THE COMING-HOME ROUTINE

I've probably lost several months of my life stomping up and down the stairs trying to leave the house but failing to locate keys, phones, or sunglasses. This can be solved with a coming-home routine.

Imagine the scene: You come through the door and you have a lot of detritus that you shed at various points throughout your home. Where do you put your keys? Where do you put your umbrella? Where do you put your gloves? Determine the best place for all these items to live, or create a space for them. I have an attractive wicker basket, for example, where my husband puts his gloves, glasses cases, headphones, and wallet. This is not for long-term storage— any extra items should be put back in their proper home; the ones you are currently using can stay.

Work on your coming-home routine until you're happy with where you put everything and run it through your head a few times. Then, if you ever find yourself struggling to find an item you've shed after coming home one day, just add this item to your routine. If you have kids, help them develop their own coming-home routines and give them designated places for their bags and other paraphernalia.

THE FOREMOST FIVE

The objects that are most regularly lost are phones, keys, glasses, pens, and jewelry, so here are some specific instructions for keeping these items safe.

Phones

Losing your phone is distressing. Finding it in the fridge, as I did once, can be doubly distressing because you realize your absentmindedness has reached whole new heights. Around three million phones are lost in America each year.[2] Let's get this figure down by:

- Installing a finding app such as Find My Phone.

- Using your lock screen to display an "If found, please contact" message or use Apple's emergency note feature.

- Never putting your phone in a back pocket or on a table in a restaurant or café.

If you do lose your phone and it's on silent, use "Find my iPhone" or "Android locate" on your computer/tablet and get your phone to "play sound" or "ring" so you can hear where it is.

Keys

Keys need a place to be. Pick one spot and stick with it. If you always leave them in a bag, be mindful that your system may be compromised if you change bags. Having keys on a length of ribbon attached to your bag's inner zipper or a clip is proof against putting them down somewhere random or leaving them behind.

Glasses (and sunglasses)

Glasses chains are a great tool, and new designs mean they're not just for the elderly. People who always wear glasses rarely lose them, but if you're an occasional glasses wearer you need to set some rules:

- Where do your glasses live when at home?

- How do they travel? In which pockets? In which bag?

- Where in your home do you use them? Make a rule that as soon as you take them off, they go in your designated safe place(s), such as a top pocket or back in the case.

MEMORY TRAINING FOR "LOSERS"

Don't buy an extra piece of technology to find missing items—it's just another thing that will run out of batteries, break after a couple of years, and gather dust. Follow this exercise to boost your memory.

- If you lose things regularly, imagine that your keys, phone, and glasses are allergic to being put down anywhere but the places you've decided upon. Close your eyes and imagine them bursting into flames and swearing angrily at you until you put them away properly. This will only work if you make this a super-memorable scene, so go to town.

- Reliving these images regularly over a few days and putting your items away safely will become habit.

Pens

As I mentioned on page 177, I have a particularly precious pen that writes for a lifetime, and I'm excited by the idea of keeping it for as long as possible. Pens were notoriously difficult for me to hold on to until last year, when I discovered the very high-tech solution of "tying a ribbon to it." The ribbon also makes the pen more distinctive, less stealable, and easier to find. You can also attach the other end to your bag for extra security. If there are certain areas where you use a pen regularly, you could also consider keeping a particular pen attached to those spots.

Jewelry

Many a piece of jewelry has been lost because it's simply fallen off. Check catches regularly and, if in doubt, don't wear it until a jeweler has looked at it. If you've inherited rings that are too big, get them resized before wearing. Very special jewelry should always be put straight back in its box, preferably in a safe if it's very precious or irreplaceable.

Place a small tray beside your bed and shower to store everyday jewelry that you're taking off in a hurry and you don't want to lose in your sleep or down the drain.

Make sure you have pictures of all your items for insurance purposes. You can register items with the police on sites such as immobilize.com.

When traveling

When traveling, carry jewelry on you if you're going to be out of sight of your luggage, and then put it in a safe when you're not wearing it. Never swim in the sea wearing precious jewelry, and when out in thief-prone areas, either take your jewelry off in advance or turn any flashy rings around so that you don't attract attention.

LOSING PRECIOUS ITEMS

I've lost a few things in my life that were precious and irreplaceable, including my first teddy bear, my first diary, and countless lovely single earrings, leaving the other one to mock me from the box. It's always painful and frustrating. Luckily, there are a few simple things we can do to help replace or find our treasures.

Digitally back up photographs and documents that mean the most to you, including old diaries and letters. Store these in a separate location or in the cloud. Make sure any art, jewelry, furniture, and bikes have been photographed. Email yourself a list with the items and how much they cost. Then make sure they are covered under insurance for fire, theft, and loss. Some insurers will even try and re-create your unique pieces so you can get back an item as close to what you lost as possible. Anything that would hurt you financially to lose should also be insured.

However, if you do lose a precious, expensive, or irreplaceable item and when you've taken all reasonable steps to find it, it's still lost, let it go. If it's gone, it's gone, and the only person who gets hurt by anguishing over it is you. If this has happened to you, try this exercise.

SAYING GOODBYE TO AN OBJECT

We can let objects have more power over us than they deserve. Yes, they can be meaningful and precious, but they can never be as meaningful as the relationships or memories they represent, and those can never be lost.

- Close your eyes, picture the object, and breathe out.

- Watch it become smaller and say good-bye to it.

- Take several long breaths and feel calm about letting it go. Repeat "It was only a thing. Only a thing."

- Picture the relationship or idea that the object represented and make that image vibrant and alive in your mind. Focus on the fact that no one can take that away from you. You have it forever.

13

On Money and Happiness

or

How to Be Happy in a Cash-Mad World

"There are people who have money,
and there are people who are rich."
—COCO CHANEL

I realize that a book about buying behavior would be glaringly incomplete if it skirted around the subject of money. So, as hard as it is for a British person to talk about, I'm dedicating this chapter to our relationship with cash. Does money really make us happy? Does retail therapy work? How much can we save through long-term buying? And on what should we spend our money to get the most happiness bang for our buck?

DOES MONEY MAKE US HAPPY?

For something that was only invented 3,000 years ago, it's strange that money has become something that feels as timeless and natural as rocks or trees. But human happiness, one must assume, has been around for hundreds of thousands of years, ever since we first brought our fuzzy butts down from trees and had enough brain cells to realize we liked sitting there, surrounded by our family and friends. Nowadays, however, many of us believe that our happiness and well-being are almost singularly tied to money, and this idea is on the rise. Between 1970 and 1998, the percentage of American students who believed that it was "very important" or "essential" to be "very well off" rose from 37 to 74 percent.[1] At the same time, a reported 90 percent of Americans are stressed about money, including millionaires.[2] For many, to aim for riches is the ultimate pilgrimage, and those who are seen to have succeeded are revered. They become our gurus. We read their biographies and make their quotes into our screensavers.

This is odd, since we know through countless scientific studies that once you have enough money to be comfortable, additional material wealth doesn't have the power to make you happier. Don't take my word for it—listen to the millionaires themselves. James Altucher, a millionaire investor and author, said of his first great financial success, "I thought if I could make 10 million dollars, then it must be too easy. In fact, I honestly thought everyone else had probably already made 11 million dollars. So then I felt poor again. I now needed 100 million dollars to be happy."[3] Here we see what happens when our external fortunes increase while our internal self-worth does not. What we learn from people like Mr. Altucher is that you must learn to be happy with how much you have *now*, because if you're not happy with that, more money won't help. There will always be one more thing you want. Money won't make you a better person either, according to Warren Buffet, whose net worth is $76 billion as of 2017.[4] He says, "Of the billionaires I have known, money just brings out the basic traits in them. If they were jerks before they had money, they are simply jerks with a billion dollars."[5] Warren Buffet is an interesting case because he's shown it's possible to be rich and not materialistic. He still lives in the same family house he bought before he made his billions.

There have been almost a thousand studies into the link between money and happiness, and they have shown that money has much less to do with happiness than something like our self-esteem might.[6] In one such study, a team of psychologists looked at the effect of the 2008 Icelandic economic collapse on some of its people. Many tried desperately to regain the money they had lost. Others became less interested in money and turned their attention to family and community life. The first group reported lower levels of well-being, the second group's levels were significantly higher.[7] A life less throwaway is about both value and values. We don't want to see hard-earned money wasted, and buying for life will actively save you money in the long run. However, it is also about refocusing on the values that truly bring happiness, and the pursuit of money is not one of them.

The big exception

There is one glaring exception to this rule. If you are in debt and living from paycheck to paycheck, it's perfectly reasonable to feel anxious about money, and the only course of action then is to explore what you can do to improve your situation.

As someone who has been in debt, I know the stomach-gnawing feeling it can give you. If you find yourself marooned on no-money island, with the loan sharks circling, there are many books and websites that can give more detailed advice.

Here are some of the most important things you can do:

- Write a budget for the month, the week, and the day and stick to it.

- Check that you're on the lowest rate of electricity, gas, and water. If not, switch.

- Can you move to a smaller/cheaper home? This may seem like extreme advice, but it comes with many surprising benefits.

- Can you live with family/take in a lodger?

- Are you getting everything you're entitled to from the government?

- Can you sell anything? Or fix or make something you can sell?

- Is there anything you spend money on that might be unnecessary? My own profligate habits, for example, include cabs, coffees, and iTunes purchases.

- Can you save money on food through clever home cooking? See CookingOnaBootstrap.com for ideas. Jack Monroe, who started this website, famously fed herself and her two-year-old on just $14 a week after she lost her job and her welfare payments were delayed by several months.

- Can you save money through coupons and savvy shopping—for example, buying food when prices are reduced?

- Is there free financial advice available to you? Financialplanningdays.org or TheSimpleDollar.com may be able to help.

- Do you have any other employment opportunities?

- Are there any courses/skills you can learn to increase your earning potential?

- Can you run a small extra business—for example, a food stall at a market, tutoring, or freelance transcribing?

  If you're in debt:

- Face up to how much you owe. Add it all up. Write it down. Work out how much you can pay back a month.

- Try to move credit card debt to a zero-interest card using a balance transfer.

- Consolidate your loans. Shop around. Can you move any loans to a cheaper form of repayment?

- Pay off the highest-interest loan first.

- Do not take out any more loans.

- If you need advice, go to www.needhelppayingbills .com/html/credit_counseling_agencies.html

Even if money is tight, it's never too early to adopt a life less throwaway mindset, as that starts with accepting and feeling grateful for what you have right now. Once you do that, any improvement is a bonus.

BUYMEONCE ON A BUDGET

One of the reasons the throwaway society started was because our thin plastic friends arrived and told us we no longer needed to save up for the things we wanted. But when we don't have to spend time saving, we don't have time to think about whether we can really afford that new piece of gym equipment or one-of-a-kind *Star Wars* memorabilia. The credit card allows impulse buying, and impulse buying beyond our means.

Credit card debt is the easiest debt to get into and I've fallen into the trap myself. In 2012, I made a couple of big purchases that I convinced myself I "needed," reasoning I would tighten my belt the next month to make up for it. That was easier said than done, and the balance rolled over the next month and the next. A few months and expensive emergencies later, I found myself almost $7,000 in debt. I managed to pay it off, but it meant missing trips, restaurants, and evenings out and making no purchases beyond groceries and bills. The day the balance went down to zero, I closed the account and felt a tremendous feeling of lightness and accomplishment. Lesson learned. The next time I had a big purchase to make (a bed), I slept on the floor for four months until I'd saved enough to buy it outright. When my new bed finally arrived and I collapsed onto it for my first night's sleep, it felt doubly sweet because of the time I'd spent waiting for it.

Credit where credit is due

Having a credit history can be important if you want a mortgage, and I don't believe that credit cards are the root of all evil, but they're best used as you might use a debit card and pay it off every month. Getting credit on bigger items such as cars, sofas, and beds can make sense, especially if it's at 0 percent interest. However, the repayments need to be carefully budgeted. If it's a stretch, don't do it. You never know when something might crop up that will squeeze you further. No sofa will make you feel comfortable if it's costing you peace of mind.

Most people imagine that they will be richer in the future; the credit card industry plays on this knowledge, so many of us are tempted to stretch our funds. Self-knowledge is key. If you can't trust yourself with a credit card, give it to a trusted loved one to help you make the occasional purchase that is paid off straightaway. This will help build up your credit rating and allow you to get a mortgage when you need one.

BuyMeOnce savings?

When you buy only the things you need and keep them for the long term, you end up being able to spend more money on them, so they can be higher quality, more luxurious items whose craftsmanship and utility bring you real pleasure every day. Longer-lasting products are more expensive upfront—there's no getting away from that. However, if chosen carefully, they will save you money in the long term.

For example, the average person spends $17.94 on 1.1 umbrellas a year.[8] Our BuyMeOnce umbrella brand, Davek, sells an umbrella with a lifetime warranty and a chip in it so you don't lose it. It costs $125; therefore, it will take 6.9 years to pay for itself. After that, the average person will be saving $17.94 a year by not buying a new umbrella. So if, for example, I lived to the average life expectancy of eighty-three, I'd save $754.19 over my lifetime. And this is just one item. Imagine if all your things were built to last and were saving you hundreds of dollars.

This isn't meant to encourage you to live beyond your means by buying things you can't afford. When you live beyond your means, you force your future self to pay for your present self, and a life less throwaway is about taking care of *all* your selves. My hope is that if the demand for long-lasting products goes up, more manufacturers will start competing on durability again. The prices on durable items will therefore come down, increasing the number of people who can afford them.

Until then, if you're on a budget and you want to make a purchase, ask yourself the following questions:

- Do I really need it?

- Can I wait to save up for it?

- Can I borrow one that will do the job while I save for one?

- Can I rent one?

- Can I get a decent one second-hand online or at an auction?

- Might I find one at a garage sale/charity shop?

- Can I wait until the winter sales (when everything is reduced the most)?

- How important is it that it's in my life this very minute?

- Does anyone selling it offer interest-free credit?

- If I budget for it, could I pay it off comfortably within a year?

- If yes, what's the lowest rate of credit I can get access to?

- Can I pay it off comfortably before the interest levels go up?

- If I had an unforeseen tragedy and lost my income, could this purchase become a dangerous burden?

MONEY AND LIFESTYLE

The course of life never runs smooth, and while in the movies the trajectory tends to be toward wealth, this doesn't always happen in reality. Fortunes can tumble, too, and part of the cruelty of the hedonic treadmill effect (the fact that we soon get used to our good fortune and then look to improve upon it) is that if our fortunes reverse and we have to go back to living more frugally, even if we were perfectly happy with that before, it seems like a disaster. Increasing our spending as soon as we get a pay rise and spending money we expect to have in the future can leave us exposed if our fortunes flounder. Another thing to consider is that if you earn big money in a job you don't enjoy, you can trap yourself in it. I know several people who ache to leave their city jobs. They're stressed and miserable and it's making them unhealthy. But their family has become used to a luxury lifestyle, so leaving doesn't feel like an option.

So, *before* you get that pay rise or higher-paid job, decide what your optimal living standard will be. The ideal is to keep your general standard of living economical and then have some treats. Everyone will interpret this differently, of course. What will be the necessities and what will be the luxuries for you? Try the exercise on the following page.

HOW TO BE HAPPY WITHOUT SHOPPING

Many of us—40 percent of women and 19 percent of men—admit that we use shopping to relieve stress and to make ourselves happier,[9] and 93 percent of teenage girls say shopping is their favorite pastime. Shopping isn't called "retail therapy" for nothing. While purchasing a product does give us a little buzz of happiness chemicals, it's a short-lived high, and if that buzz is being used to try and self-medicate for some underlying unhappiness, then it's not the right cure and the underlying unhappiness will continue. I think we self-medicate with shopping because happiness is often confused with pleasure. Pleasure is a momentary experience felt by the short-term part of our brains, but it's very possible to have a pleasurable experience and still be deeply miserable.

Happiness is more than just the presence of pleasure. It is controlled by the story we tell ourselves about our life, and the good news is that we can change our story. For example, upon finding out you failed to get a job, the story running in your head could be "I'm such a loser for goofing off and binge-watching that boxset instead of prepping properly. My partner's not going to want to be with a loser like me. She's probably thinking of leaving." Instead, it could be "This is really embarrassing. I didn't work hard enough. But I'm going to learn from this and put a plan in place so it doesn't happen again. What can I do tonight with my partner to cheer us up?" How you think about yourself is entirely up to you. Even if you think you have proof that you've been a loser in the past (and *everyone* has this proof), you can draw a delicious, fresh line in the sand at any point and change your story.

PRIORITIZING WHERE YOUR MONEY GOES

Here's a list of the twenty main "luxuries"/priorities we choose to spend money on. Rank them from 1 to 20, with 1 being the most important to you and 20 the least. If you have trouble choosing, say to yourself, "I'd rather spend money on X than on Y, and see if it rings true. Shuffle them around a few times if need be and see what feels right to you.

I've left off things that we don't have much choice over, such as medical bills, insurance, basic food and shelter, clothing, and hygiene.

- Location of home
- Decor, furniture, and home environment
- Good food and drink
- Socializing
- Fitness, sports, and hobbies
- Books, films, and music
- Cultural activities (museums/theatre)
- Clothing, accessories and shoes
- Beauty products and personal grooming
- Gambling

- Vacations and trips

- Working less

- Fulfilling work

- Toys, gadgets, and tech

- Gardening/yardwork

- Cars or other transport

- More room in the house for guests

- Extra insurance

- Presents

- Recreational drugs and cigarettes

Now, look at your priorities and, next to each one, write what you think you're currently spending per month on them; apart from "working less" and "fulfilling work," in which case estimate what your income would be if you did those things and what a difference in salary that would be. Indicate with an arrow whether you would like your spending to go up or down for each item. Put a date in your diary to reappraise this list in a year's time.

Are you spending according to your priorities? Try to keep any spending in the future focused on the top of your list to ensure that your lifestyle reflects what you find important.

Your partner may have different priorities from you, and that's absolutely fine. Sit down with them and make a list together. Don't sweat it if they are a bit different, but if there are major differences, it can be worth discussing them in a calm, compassionate, and understanding way.

This self-awareness and control over your inner voice is a powerful tool, but it isn't the only tool we have for well-being. From all the research I've done, the following are what I've identified as the core pillars of a happy life:

- A sense of freedom and autonomy (control over your life)

- Deep relationships

- A sense of belonging and community

- A sense of growth (that things are getting better)

- Gratitude

- Purpose and passion

- Self-worth/self-control

- A calm, comfortable, and revitalizing environment to live in

This book will not only help you with the last and arguably least important of these pillars, but it will also help realign your life to make the others easier to achieve as well. Here are some quick practical exercises to get you thinking and excited about each of the pillars on this list, and there's a Further Reading section at the back of the book should you want to explore any of these (or other) subjects in greater depth.

A sense of freedom and autonomy

Many of us feel trapped by circumstances, and this feeling often comes from trying to control things that are out of our hands. All we ever have true control over is our own actions and thoughts. But this is enough. Even if we are incarcerated, there are certain freedoms that can't be taken from us. As Viktor E. Frankl, formerly an Auschwitz prisoner, stated,

"Everything can be taken from a man but one thing: the last of the human freedoms—to choose one's attitude in any given set of circumstances, to choose one's own way."[10]

FIND YOUR FREEDOMS

Take responsibility for what you *can* change in your life. Write a list of what you have the power to do and control. You'll probably find that it is more than enough to be getting on with. Think of things like:

- Your actions and reactions toward others
- Your actions and thoughts toward yourself
- How you choose to spend your time
- Your goals and what you focus on
- Many aspects of your environment
- With whom you choose to spend time
- With how you express yourself

Deep relationships

The results of the longest-running study on human behavior and happiness, conducted by Harvard University for over seventy- five years, are absolutely conclusive, "Good relationships keep us happier and healthier. Period."[11] A deep connection to family, friends, and community has huge health benefits—more than any other lifestyle factor, including cholesterol levels or income. On the flip side, lonely people's brains and bodies start to decline earlier, whereas people in happy relationships are protected from brain-declining memory loss.[12]

To foster deep relationships, we have to connect properly with the people we care for. There's no substitute for face-to-face time; the chemicals that fire in our brains don't happen when we put technology in between us. Video chat is the next best thing but a friendship can't live by text alone.

CONNECT WITH YOUR SPECIAL PEOPLE

Make sure you make time to see your special people (you know who they are) as regularly as you can. Building traditions such as a boys' night on the first Friday of the month or an annual extended family weekend can help with the hectic schedules everyone seems to keep nowadays. It's the quality, not the quantity, of the relationships that matter. Therefore, we should work to create more empathy and love in the relationships we already have rather than seeking to have many shallower relationships. Feeling close to people means sharing our vulnerabilities to help create understanding. One study found that even strangers who asked and answered increasingly personal questions and engaged in eye contact could very quickly feel a deep sense of connection and even love for each other.[13]

Try this with your friends and family, using the questions you'll find at 36questionsinlove.com. Play it like a game, with each person getting a chance to ask and answer. Then hold eye contact for three minutes. What's wonderful about this exercise is that the questions can bring up some real surprises. I played this game with my dad and found out all sorts of things that I didn't know, from his ultimate dinner guest (David Attenborough) and his favorite feeling (jamming with a band) to what he's most grateful for in his life (his children).

A sense of belonging and community

Humans are built to live in tribes or villages, but the current rise of individualism means that we are much less community-minded nowadays; we think predominantly about our own lives. This new culture, alongside the realities of having to work, make money, and raise children in our little nuclear families, means that we are getting worse at connecting with other members of society. It's perhaps no surprise that one in five people admit that they are lonely.[14] Feeling a connection to those who came before us can help give us a sense of belonging, so ask the oldest member of your family all about your relatives. Record the conversation if possible. That way, one day, your grandchildren's grandchildren can also feel connected to the people from whom they are descended.

You can foster belonging by seeing a group of friends or people with shared interests more regularly and letting the relationships within those groups deepen by sharing and responding to personal information. Also, try to reach out and get involved in your local community in some way, as this can make you feel safer and more comfortable in your area, and this peace of mind can only add to your overall sense of well-being.

FIND YOUR TRIBE

Wherever you live, there will be people with whom you can find a common cause. It doesn't have to be many people either. By all means, use the internet to find them but meet in person if you want to feel the benefits of belonging.

A sense of growth

To feel happy, we need a sense that things are getting better or will get better. I think this is because as soon as you have growth, you have a story, which your mind recognizes.

It projects into the future and sees an upward trend and is happy. Gretchen Rubin, author of *The Happiness Project*, wrote about how in later life her dad gave up tennis to focus on golf, because his tennis was getting worse but his golf was improving, which made him much happier.

GROW EVERY DAY

Decide what growth you're going to bring into your life each day. You could decide:

- To learn something new (for example, another song on the guitar)

- To grow a relationship

- To grow a skill

- To grow a body of work (from knitting a scarf to writing your magnum opus)

- To grow your garden

- To grow your kid's experiences

- To grow your own experience of the world

Gratitude

Gratitude is good for us for many reasons, but it's especially powerful as an antidote to that ultimate killer of happiness—comparing ourselves to others—something that has become an epidemic in the world of social media. A University of Michigan study found that the more people used Facebook, the less life satisfaction they had.[15] This is because when everyone shows us the bright moments of their lives, ours can feel drab in comparison, and this can lead to all sorts of agony. Or we might decide that we're better off and feel superior, which isn't necessarily good for us either. You can create immunity from comparison and envy through gratitude for what you do have and the knowledge that you can never truly know if someone is having a better time than you are. There are rich, "successful," talented, and deeply loved people who are desperately unhappy, and there are poor, sick, and even dying people who have a profound inner joy. The great thing is that this is all within your control. You might not be able to control a lot in your life, but often you can control how you feel about it.

TELL YOURSELF A BETTER STORY

In the morning and evening, find at least one thing (preferably three) that you can feel grateful for. To give you an example, mine this morning were:

1. I'm grateful that the gym is so close.

2. I'm grateful that my little rose tree is about to bloom.

3. I'm grateful that my husband could work from home today.

On top of that, here are some mantras to try. Just say them over and over to yourself:

- I have chosen the life I have and I am choosing well.

- I need very little to be happy.

- I appreciate all the lovely people and things I have in my life.

- Nothing anyone else has can make me feel bad about my life.

Instead of telling yourself, "My life isn't good enough until I get X, or until Y happens," change your story to "I'm so lucky, I'm the kind of person who needs very little to be happy." This is a powerful story and you can take pride in it. It's even a true story. You might think, isn't this a bit unmotivating? There is an argument that you should "stay hungry"—that if you're satisfied with your lot, you might just languish and get bored. But if you're already happy with what you have materially, then what you do in life will be for the joy of doing it and you can "stay hungry" for the things that matter to you most—solving a challenge, creating something brilliant, helping others, increasing understanding, or taking pride in doing something well. And this will lead to even more satisfaction.

Purpose and passion

We went deep into finding your purpose in chapter 7, but a way to discover what you truly care about is to watch where your brain goes when it's allowed to go anywhere.

HAVE A PURPOSEFUL WEEKEND

If you constantly keep your brain occupied with your mobile phone, music, radio, or TV, then give yourself a weekend without any of your usual distractions. Keep a notebook handy and jot down what you find yourself thinking about. If you're drawing a blank, try writing five endings to the sentence "I've often wondered. . . ."

Pick an answer that resonates with you and start following that trail; you don't know where it might lead. It could lead to your purpose and passion. It might go nowhere, but nothing is lost in the pursuit of interesting things.

Self-worth and self-control

So many people treat themselves in a way they'd never dream of treating a friend or someone they cared about. One of my favorite thinkers on self-esteem, Elizabeth Gilbert, would ask, "What makes you so special that you among all the creatures of this earth are not deserving of compassion?"

The important word here is "compassion." We're looking to be compassionate toward ourselves, not worship ourselves. Having self-esteem doesn't mean we should feel superior to anyone else or entitled to anything. It simply means that we recognize that we're worthy of respect and kindness from ourselves. If we know that in our bones, almost everything on Earth becomes easier to deal with.

BE A FRIEND TO YOURSELF

Be a friend to yourself, and I mean literally. Here are some ideas.

Affirmations

Start doing affirmations every morning. When I first heard about this, I thought it sounded corny, lame, and embarrassing, but I still tried it. It felt as awkward as hell stating peppy thoughts in the mirror, but it really worked. I told myself things like "You enjoy eating fresh, healthful food every day" and this little voice stayed with me while I was resisting a McDonald's apple pie.

So, tell yourself you're already behaving/feeling the way you want to feel—for example, "I am full of energy," "I am patient," "I am confident"—and see what happens.

continued

Also, just be nice to yourself. For example, you can affirm "Whatever happens today, you are good enough and I love you."

Look Through Another's Eyes

Just as you did earlier (see page 146), imagine looking at yourself through the eyes of someone who thinks well of you.

Trust Yourself

Self-esteem is highly linked to self-trust. If you feel you have let yourself down in the past, learning to trust yourself again can be a slow process. So, start small. Make tiny promises to yourself each morning and keep them. They can even be promises you know you'll keep. Anything from "I promise to make my bed today" to "I promise to treat myself to a slice of cake for dessert." Before you go to bed, thank yourself for keeping those promises. In time, once you start to trust that you'll keep promises, start demanding more of yourself—"I promise to apply for a new job" or "I promise to get up earlier to exercise." Before long you'll have built up a deep and lasting faith in yourself, and even if you make mistakes, as everyone does, it won't damage your self-belief.

A calm, comfortable, and revitalizing environment

When you've bought quality for the long term and in accordance with your values, your home will naturally become more of a haven and less of a source of stress. Living a life less throwaway will directly help with this.

> **IMPROVING YOUR HOME'S MOOD**
>
> As an added check, monitor your mood this week as you walk into each room of your house. How does each one make you feel? Is there anything you can do immediately to help make a room feel more inviting, calm, comfortable or exciting?
>
> Write down longer-term goals for your home, starting from how you want to feel when you're in each room, and then work out how that might be accomplished.

I hope that some of these suggestions and exercises are useful in a small way. For more ideas, see the Further Reading section. It's clear that most of our happiness is completely unrelated to how much money we have, but are there certain types of spending that are better than others?

WHAT SPENDING MAKES US HAPPIEST?

In an experiment run by the Harvard Business School, a group of people were given a certain amount of money to spend either on themselves or on others, and their moods were monitored. It was found that those who had given the money to charity or other people still had an elevated mood several hours later, while those who had simply gone shopping had no rise in mood at all by the end of the day.[16] In fact, giving money to others has been conclusively proven to make us happier than treating ourselves.[17] If you want a piece of this happiness action, choose a particular charity each year that you're going to help. Give regularly in amounts you can afford and bask in the warm glow it gives you.

After selfless giving, all the evidence tells us that spending money on experiences is the way to go.

Why experiences, not goods?

In his excellent book *Stuffocation*, James Wallman makes a passionate and highly informed argument for why choosing experiences over material goods increases happiness.[18] His five main points, all backed by scientific research, are essentially:

- When we make a bad buying decision, that material item hangs around, making us feel bad about it. But even when we have a bad experience, we often look back, laugh, and end up feeling positive about it. "Remember when the airline lost our suitcase and Mom had to wear Dad's clothes?"

- Material possessions get "old" in our mind; they are exciting at first but we soon get bored with them and crave something else. With experiences, this doesn't happen.

- We might worry about making the right choice when it comes to a material item, but we worry less about making the right choice when it comes to an experience. There is also less judgment from other people on the experiences we choose to have than the material items we choose to buy.

- Experiences, rather than goods, are better at defining who we are.

- Experiences bring us closer to other people. When we share an experience or an activity with someone, we're more likely to feel connected to them.

I would also add:

- Experiences help us live more in the moment.

- They help us know ourselves better.

- They keep us curious and connected to the world.

- We look forward to experiences more than to buying material things because they create happiness even when they're not happening.

- We get more happiness when we look forward to a nice experience, than having a nice material item.[19]

- It's also been shown that spending money on services to give ourselves more free time promotes happiness. [20]

And there are, of course, some objects that continue to give us great experiences, and these are the objects we should be investing in. I think if I bought my car just to own a nice car, then the thrill would soon have worn off. However, because it's a convertible and feeling the wind on my face as I drive is one of my favorite feelings, it turns every trip into an adventure and continues to bring me truly heavenly experiences, even if they come with a side order of fright hair.

Conclusion

or

What Does Success Look Like in a Life Less Throwaway?

A great designer and a great man, Victor Papanek, warned us as far back as 1971 that throwing away furniture, cars, clothing, and appliances might soon lead us to feel that marriages and other personal relationships were throwaway items as well, and that on a global scale, countries and, indeed, entire subcontinents were as disposable as Kleenex.[1] The smallest goal of this book was to help you clear the superfluous and be empowered to start bringing into your life a curation of not perfect but "perfect for you" pieces—objects that have been picked mindfully with both your present and future self in mind. When brought together in your home, they should help create a lasting sanctuary, somewhere you can be completely comfortable and unabashedly "you."

The bigger goal is that this book might help to shift the relationship you have with material things and yourself. Right now, an alien looking down at the planet might easily assume that the purpose of humans is for each of us to get as much stuff as possible over our lifetimes, like some kind of giant game of Hungry Hungry Hippos. One thing that surprised me most when writing this book was discovering just how much of what we see and hear every day is slyly trying to persuade us that this is what our purpose should be—that our lives will be richer, fuller, and more meaningful if we have this or that or live a life that looks like another person's Instagram account. It often takes people right until the end of their lives to realize what an illusion material possessions are. With luck, this book will have given you a head start and a shield you can pick up any time you want to stand firm against these pressures.

A life less throwaway, while simpler in many ways, isn't necessarily the easiest life. This isn't because it's hard to do on a practical level but because the majority of society is so wedded to rampant consumerism that it's liable to suck us back into its clammy folds if we're not tough enough to resist it. Remember, you can go back and redo the exercises as regularly as you want. Better still, teach them to other people; this is proven to be one of the best ways to ensure you take something in fully.

This book may or may not have crystallized what purpose and success mean to you. If you're still searching, look for role models who are living their lives mindfully. One of mine, Bill Watterson, creator of the brilliant *Calvin and Hobbes* cartoon strip, was under constant pressure to make merchandise out of the characters—Hobbes cuddly toys and Calvin bumper stickers—but he realized that by doing so, his purpose for writing would shift from creativity to selling things, his characters would lose their voices, and then the money he earned would have to supply all the meaning he needed. In his speech to his alma mater in 1990, he gave the following advice to students:

"With each decision, we tell ourselves and the world who we are. Think about what you want out of this life and recognize that there are many kinds of success. Creating a life that reflects your values and satisfies your soul is a rare achievement. In a culture that relentlessly promotes avarice and excess as the good life, a person happy doing his own work is usually considered an eccentric, if not a subversive."[2]

This is what success looks like to me. To invent your own life's meaning isn't easy, but it's still allowed, and I believe we'll all be happier for it.

LOOKING AHEAD

But won't buying for life break the economy?

One of the defenses I get for fast fashion and throwaway culture is that all the rampant production stimulates the economy. So will the economy collapse if we all start buying for life? In short, no, it will evolve. In the same way that people no longer spend their money on horses and carriages, with mindful curation they won't be spending their money on throwaway objects but on more durable ones, and on servicing and repairing them. People will undoubtedly save money by buying for life and may find themselves with more disposable income. This will go to one of three places: either it will be spent on services and experiences, such as going out for dinner more regularly and enjoying hobbies, or it will be invested in companies so that they can grow and prosper, or it will be saved. More money saved means that there will be more money for banks to invest in infrastructure, sustainable power, and solutions to the problems we face.

The brightest companies will move toward what is known as a "circular economy model" where nothing is wasted. Products are made using sustainable and recycled and recyclable materials, and are designed to last as long as they can and be useful to as many people as possible. Many companies may move to the rental model, such as "car sharing" and Rent the Runway dresses. If we start now, our economy can naturally and gradually evolve, allowing industries, companies, and their associated jobs to adapt over time. This is a much better scenario than waiting until a crisis forces a sudden change in the job market. At the moment, the economy is set up so that it's only stable if it's growing. Governments therefore do all they can to encourage us to keep calm and carry on shopping with little thought as to whether this serves our long-term well-being and happiness or the health of the planet. Because governments are short-term entities, they have little incentive to put through policies that only bear fruit in the long term.

In his book *Prosperity without Growth*, Professor Tim Jackson offers an alternative. He asks us to reframe what prosperity means. It need not mean a yacht and a villa in the south of France; it can be the feeling of well-being that comes from being part of a flourishing community. Inequality breeds resentment and mistrust within society. Imagine living in a village of one hundred people and one villager keeps half the money while many of the others starve. This is the reality of the world right now, and the gap between rich and poor is vast and growing. As the rich tend to make the rules of the game, the game is more firmly rigged in their favor.

Restructuring our economy on a fair and sustainable model that doesn't depend on a constant increase in the resources we use will take hard work, imagination, and bravery. It will need enlightened governments, businesses, and community leaders to communicate the vision of how life could be—less materialistic, more equal, more collaborative; green, sustainable, and happy. This isn't a pipe dream. The societies that are closest to this model, in Norway and Denmark, have some of the highest happiness levels in the world.

What's at stake?

It's been estimated that if everyone in the world lived like we do in the West, we would need about four Earths to survive.[3] Furthermore, countries in Asia, Africa, and South America are quickly catching up and emulating our lifestyle. We urgently need to move to ways of living that don't rely on perpetual consumption and growth, not only so that we don't run out of resources but so that we can save the world from the effects of climate change.

The earth has already heated by 0.8°C since the late nineteenth century. I watched with disbelief and anguish as the forty-fifth president of the United States pulled out of the Paris climate accord. This agreement aims to keep the world from warming more than 2°C, but even at 1.5°C we're going to see some catastrophic effects.[4] Saleemul Huq, director of the International Centre for Climate Change and Development in Bangladesh, a country already feeling the effects of climate change, warns that "the consequences of failing to keep the temperature below a 1.5°C rise will be to willfully condemn hundreds of millions of the poorest citizens of Earth to certain deaths from the severe impacts of climate change."[5]

If global warming continues as it is, we will lose the ice caps and then sea levels will rise by as much as 216 feet. Temperatures, even in temperate places like Britain, could reach 45°C (113°F), causing tarmac and electric cabling to melt. Much of Africa will be uninhabitable due to the heat. We will lose whole countries such as Denmark and the Maldives, and great and beautiful cities like Venice will become Atlantis-style myths. A third of our fresh water will disappear, and seawater will inundate the entire east coasts of America and Australia, including New York, Boston, the whole of Florida, Sydney, and Brisbane.[6] It's generally agreed now that we will smash through the 2°C target and reach the 4°C barrier by 2100 at the latest.[7] My husband and I are hoping for children, and this will be within their lifetime.

But there is hope. We are that hope. Half of global emissions are due to just 10 percent of people.[8] That includes me and probably you too. Instead of feeling guilty, this should make us feel empowered, because what we choose to do can have the biggest impact. A high-consuming individual or family in the West deciding to live a life less throwaway makes a much bigger dent in CO_2 emissions than someone who already lives simply. Thousands of years ago, we as a species were programmed to be fair and helpful to our home tribe and protective and competitive toward the tribes around us. Nowadays, our tribe has shrunk to the nuclear family, or sometimes just ourselves. But at the same time we are reliant on the whole human and natural ecosystem. Our tribe, whether we like it or not, is the whole world. Due to the fragile nature of the planet, we will live or die together. We can't just rely on our governments or scientists to save us. If we want a future for our children and grandchildren, I believe we must take things into our own hands.

If you are an individual: Follow the methods in this book, make the change and spread the message as often as you can without becoming a bore at parties. Join the community at BuyMeOnce.com and help us spread the message globally.

If you run a company: Please get in touch. There's so much we could do together.

If you are a cat: Keep doing that. Great job.

A STORY TO END

When I was seven, my best friend and I would sit in the school library and scheme about how we could "save all the animals." Determined to have our message heard, we invented a "projector" out of my father's flashlight, a cardboard box, and cut-out letters stuck onto transparent tape, and managed to beam "Save the World" onto my pink bedroom walls.

Elated, we thought that if we found a light bright enough, we might be able to project this message onto the moon. Then, miraculously, people would stop polluting, start recycling, and we would literally have saved the world. Sadly, when it came to projecting onto the moon, even my dad's biggest flashlight didn't quite cut it.

Two decades later, as a rather unhappy woman working in advertising, I had the idea for BuyMeOnce, but resisted it for months. I didn't know how to build a website, let alone run my own business. Finally, I asked myself, "If it never makes any money, do you still want it to exist?" And when the answer was "Yes," suddenly everything was much simpler. When a journalist found me on Twitter and asked if she could write about what I was doing, I didn't feel ready to launch, but I also knew that I'd probably never feel ready to launch. In January 2016, an article called "The Rise of BuyMeOnce Shopping" was published in the United Kingdom's *Telegraph* and my world went crazy. Suddenly, everyone was looking. I couldn't open my e-mails as fast as they were coming in.

Since then, BuyMeOnce has moved from my kitchen table to an office with seven amazing team members. As of 2017, more than two million people have visited the site, and people from all over the planet have contacted us asking how they can help. My dream is that BuyMeOnce becomes a community, a tribe of like-minded people who are willing to stand up to shoddiness, break the rules, build the best products, and throw away our throwaway culture.

So you see, I found my flashlight. And that light was an idea so strong it wouldn't let me go, an idea so clear that a child can understand it, and so bright the world is looking up and seeing it. The way we buy things is broken and the things we buy are breaking. But we can break this cycle. If we buy things we love, buy things that last, and take care of them, we might just save the world.

Thank you for reading.

Ten Steps to
Mastering Mindful Curation

1. Understand the manipulations ranged against you that promote mindless consumerism rather than mindful curation.

2. Use the proscribed techniques to free yourself from external manipulations so that you are free to make mindful choices.

3. Find your purpose.

4. Identify your long-term priorities that will help you meet this purpose.

5. Identify what items you need to fulfill those priorities and to live comfortably without being unduly influenced by status concerns.

6. Identify your core tastes and sense of style and what suits you.

7. Identify your values and the brands that reflect those same values.

8. Take stock of the items you have to inform your present taste, priorities, and buying habits.

9. Let go of the superfluous and identify what you do not need.

10. Choose each new item with your previously identified long-term priorities and tastes in mind.

Care and Repair

This is not an exhaustive manual, but should help you care for the majority of items in your home. I recommend supplementing it with online videos from manufacturers and the public that give clear visual instructions for some of the following methods here (just don't get sidetracked by the cats). Here's a list for quick reference.

HOUSEHOLD MAINTENANCE

I've written the following list to help you with the maintenance tasks that will have the most impact on the longevity of your belongings.

Every day

Act fast to clean up spills on furniture or clothing.
Update software as needed to avoid getting hacked.

Every week

Vacuum, dust, and clean the house and furniture.
Condition regularly worn shoes.
Clean clothes as necessary.
Clean out the dishwasher filter.

Every month

Descale the coffee maker (see page 265).
Condition regularly used leather bags and shoes
    worn less often.
Fix any garments in the mending pile.

Every three months

Oil wood cutting boards and spoons.
Put frozen vinegar cubes in the garbage disposal.
Check the smoke alarms.
Check the water softener (if you have one).

Every six months

Deep clean the house.
Turn and vacuum the mattress.
Launder the pillows and duvet.
Polish wood furniture.
Deep clean the fridge.
Clean the refrigerator coils. Put petroleum jelly
    on the fridge seals.

Run the cleaning cycle of the dishwasher and washing machine.

Inspect the gutters.

Every year

Take stock of the items in your life (see Chapter 8).

Have any leather jackets professionally cleaned.

Get the knives sharpened.

Clean the filter in the kitchen hood fan.

Check the grouting around the tiles in the kitchen and bathroom. Flush the hot-water system and have the boiler serviced.

Inspect the roof and exterior of your home (best done in spring/summer).

Fix any loose fixings or screws.

Clean and consider repainting/resealing the exterior woodwork.

Every two years

Have a professional deep clean of your upholstery and carpets.

CARING FOR LEATHER PRODUCTS

Leather is a durable material that ages gracefully—but only if it's taken care of. Always ask the people who made your leather product what the best care for it is. I suggest the following.

- Spray the item with a water repellent when you first get it.

- Use a gentle hand or face soap to remove general grime.

- Brush off any mud or dust with a short brush and then wipe it with a thoroughly wrung-out cloth.

- Condition it with an oil or cream conditioner.

- Use a couple of cloths (old T-shirts work well) to buff the polish on in small circles, then buff off with another cloth.

- Polishing, even with clear leather polish, may change the color slightly, so try it out on a small area that isn't seen first.

- If you're using a bag every day, clean, condition, and polish it every two weeks.

- Clean, condition, and polish your shoes regularly—at least every ten wears if you want them to last. If they are particularly precious, condition and polish them every time you wear them.

- Clean and condition garments as needed. As well as using soap, you can steam them and wipe them with a wrung-out cloth. If they are favorites, have a professional clean once a year.

- For pen marks on clothes or upholstery, try hair spray or rubbing alcohol on them.

Accidents and stains

Water can stain leather badly, but if you do have a spill, blot it up as soon as possible with a clean cloth or towel and let the leather dry naturally. Direct heat, such as a hair dryer, can dry it out.

Leather can scratch too, so be mindful when you're walking not to scuff your shoes against rough objects or snag your bag on anything sharp or spiky.

Stains on suede

Brush gently with a suede brush, first in one direction and then in another. If they are water stains and they aren't removed when you first brush them, mist lightly with water and re-brush gently while wet.

Leather storage

No leather likes to be stored at extreme temperatures—hot or cold—or in direct sunlight. All can fade or damage it.

Bags

Don't store leather or suede bags in airtight boxes or bags; they need to breathe or they may go moldy. Use a fabric dust bag or a pillowcase to protect the bag and make sure it's stored in a way that doesn't squash or fold the leather, as that is how permanent cracks form.

Shoes

Some people store shoes in their original boxes and this is certainly a good idea with particularly special formal shoes.

Wooden shoetrees will help keep the shape of special shoes, or you can stuff the shoes with tissue paper. (Both options also absorb any extra moisture that could be lingering in the shoe.)

Don't leave shoes out on racks exposed to sunlight and dust, as both are life-shortening for leather. Lay shoes out at the bottom of your closet, in a shoe cupboard, or in drawers.

Leather jackets

Make sure they've been cleaned before storing them for the summer. Stuff some old tissue paper or newspaper inside the arms to stop them from collapsing. Hang each jacket on a wide, chunky hanger in a garment bag or an old sheet.

CARING FOR CLOTHES AND FABRICS

If you're dismayed by the amount of handwashing involved with delicate fabrics, I'd steer you toward buying cotton, bamboo, or lyocell. Wash all your clothes as coolly and with as little detergent as you can (experiment to see what works for you) and air-dry them if possible, as tumble drying can fade and shrink them and uses up huge amounts of energy.

Washing

You may find you need to wash clothes less often than you think. Wear them on rotation so that they have time to air and breathe between wears, and if a garment doesn't look dirty or smell dirty, don't automatically throw it in the wash just because it's been worn. The less you wash it, the longer it will last.

This is doubly true for dry-cleaning. If you can get away with a bit of spot cleaning rather than sending the whole garment in to be cleaned, that's a much better option.

On the other hand, if your clothes are wet and sweaty, wash them sooner rather than later, as they can go moldy, which can stain and damage the fabric.

Always read the washing instructions and turn everything inside out before putting it in the machine (this helps to prevent the pilling of woolens and fading of printed patterns), and put more delicate items in a mesh bag.

When ironing, be sure to set the iron to the correct temperature, as many a garment has met its end this way. If you're not sure a fabric can be ironed and want to play it safe, remember that many wrinkles will drop out if you hang a garment in a steamy bathroom.

Swimwear and delicate underwear

Be sure to rinse out your swimwear after every pool or beach trip. You only need to hand wash it with detergent every few wears. This will help it last longer. Don't stretch the fabric by wringing it out; simply squeeze it and place it flat to dry indoors (sun can damage it).

Lacy, delicate underwear should be hand washed and rinsed out well. Be sure to separate lights from darks, as white delicates are particularly prone to picking up any dye that bleeds out of darker colors.

Cashmere

Cashmere is a glorious fabric but very delicate, so wash it as rarely as possible by hand in cool water with a wool-friendly cleaner. Dry flat so it doesn't stretch.

Cotton

Machine wash on hot and rinse twice for optimum softness. To restore whites, add bleach. You can iron up to the highest temperature if needed.

Denim

Spot clean your jeans if you can, as washing can make them lose their shape. You can pop them in the freezer to get rid of bacteria. Very occasionally, pull them inside out on a delicate wash or wash them in the bathtub, and be sure to wash separately, as they can damage your other clothes. Adding a cup of white wine vinegar will help keep them dark. Don't put them in the dryer, as that will break down their fibers and they will lose their shape over time.

Polyester

Machine wash on warm and iron on medium.

Rayon

Wash on cold and hang immediately to minimize wrinkles. Use a medium iron.

Silk

Hand wash silk in cool water and go easy with the detergent, which should be as mild as possible. Add a few tablespoons of vinegar to the water to keep the color vibrant and the silk in good condition. Don't wring it out, as this can damage it. You can also dry-clean silk, but this can get costly. Iron with a cool iron while it is still slightly wet.

Velvet

Most velvet needs to be dry-cleaned, but not all. Never iron or fold it, as the creases will become permanent lines. If it's wrinkled, use a steamy bathroom or hand steamer if you have one.

Wool

Either machine wash on the wool setting or hand wash. If you hand wash, make sure the water is cool, otherwise the wool will clump and shrink. Dry flat.

Storing

When storing clothes, you can fold or roll many of them in drawers (making sure they are stacked vertically so you can see every item on opening the drawer). For the items that require hanging, use decent hangers that protect the clothes from becoming misshapen and protect your sanity from a tangle of wire hangers. Never pack your clothes too tightly together, as they need to breathe. Any heavy fabrics should be hung on wide hangers so they don't lose their shape at the shoulders.

If you're storing clothes for the season, make sure they are clean, then wrap them in clean cotton sheets and store in a dry place. Add some moisture absorbers if you live in a humid climate. You don't want them to smell like mold in six months' time.

To store precious items for years, use a professional, acid-free garment storage box. Natural fibers (cotton, linen, wool, and silk) need air, so only vacuum-pack man-made fibers.

Other Storage Tips

Cashmere: Roll or hang it and keep a few moth-repelling cedar balls in your closet to make sure you don't come back to a holey mess *(see "Preventing moths," below)*. Never store it in plastic, but do use a garment bag if you're putting it away for the season.

Jeans: Always hang or roll your jeans rather than fold them, as they will weaken at the fold points.

Silk: Store out of direct sunlight, which can make it brittle.

Wool: Store rolled or folded, as hanging can stretch the knitting, and use moth-preventing measures *(see below)*.

Preventing moths: Keep your clothes smelling fantastic and keep moths at bay at the same time with a light spray of diluted lavender essence. Cedar balls are also effective. Unfortunately, moths have very good taste and tend to go for the expensive natural fabrics first, so if you suspect that you have moths, freeze your most precious pieces of clothing in a plastic bag for a couple of days to kill the moths. Cashmere, wool, silk, and cotton are the most at risk.

Maintaining

Once you have invested in your capsule wardrobe (see page 90), you need to invest in the time to care for it so it will last as long as possible.

Faded clothes

You can give clothes a new lease on life by dyeing them. If an outfit looks faded and worn and you're thinking of letting it go, see if you can restore it to its former glory.

Outerwear

Use a clothes brush or lint brush to pick up dirt and pet hair. Avoid sending coats to the dry-cleaners unnecessarily by spot cleaning and airing them.

Pilled clothes

Because of pilling, many people get rid of their clothes when it's not necessary. Pilling can be banished using a few techniques:

- Wash the garment. Put it on once dry. Pass a razor over it as if you were shaving yourself very gently. Try a small area first until you grow in confidence.

- Use a Velcro hair roller to pick up the pilling.

- Use a lint shaver.

Shrunken clothes

If something has shrunk in the wash, keep it damp and very gently stretch it out again. Put it on while wet (it might feel horrible but could save a sweater's life) and stroke, tease, and pull the fabric back into place before it dries.

REPAIRING CLOTHES

Even when you do your best to maintain your garments, accidents still happen. Know the basics of simple repairs so you don't have to send out an easy job.

Patching

- Don't use an iron-on patch unless you plan to reinforce it with stitching, as they can start to peel after a few washes.

- Cut a patch that is ½ inch wider than the hole you're covering. The patch can be any shape, but bear in mind that a more irregular one will be harder to sew. Use either the same fabric or a clashing fabric if you want to make a statement. You can often find spare fabric within the garment, either in a seam or the inside of a pocket.

- Pin the patch in place around the edges of the hole. Try to match the grain of the patch to the fabric if you want it to blend in.

- Pick a thread as close to the color of the fabric as you can and sew it in place as close to the edges of the patch as possible.

- Use a zigzag or straight stitch on the sewing machine or a backstitch if you are hand sewing. Tie off the thread on the inside of the fabric and tidy up any fraying.

Darning a small knitwear or cotton hole

- Take some thread that is the same color as the wool and catch a strand of wool on one edge of the hole, then catch another strand on the opposite side.

- Slowly and carefully, start drawing the strands together, being careful not to pull them too tight.

- Keep going around the edge of the hole until the strands are brought together and the hole is no longer visible.

Darning a medium knitwear or cotton hole

- Make a running stitch all around the hole to keep it from stretching.

- Place a darning mushroom or a curved surface, such as the side of a bowl or cup, under the hole to keep the fabric stable.

- Make several small stitches, one over the other, to secure your thread, then stitch across the hole horizontally, as if creating miniature cotton rungs of a ladder. (For width between the stitches, take your cue from the weave of the fabric you're darning.)

- Stitch vertically from top to bottom of the hole, weaving through the rungs you've just created.

- Tie the thread off.

Larger knitwear holes

For large holes, I recommend sewing on an appliqué patch. When my favorite sweater had been munched by mice and there seemed no way to repair it, I bought some very pretty white butterfly patches and used them to cover the holes. I love my sweater even more now for its individuality.

Sewing on buttons

Many garments come with spare buttons that we either ignore or store in a completely random way. Keep them all together, but do keep the buttons of the different people in your family separated to avoid pawing through dozens at a time. To sew on a button:

- Take a couple of feet of thread and double it up. (If you have less thread than this, don't double it.) Knot the end.

- Place the button where you want it and start sewing through the holes from the inside. Don't pull the thread completely tight or the button will be hard to thread through its hole. Allow a needle-width gap between the button and the fabric.

- Once you've done six stitches (or it looks similar to the other buttons on the garment), take the thread between the button and the fabric and wrap it tightly around the stitches you've already done.

- Finish off with a small knot on the inside of the garment.

Hemming

Sometimes the only thing keeping an item of clothing from being perfect is the length of a sleeve, leg, or skirt. Since it is unlikely you will grow to fit the garment, shorten it to fit you.

- Take up a hem by cutting the fabric to the length you want, leaving an extra inch for the new hem.

- Secure the raw edge with a zigzag stitch on the sewing machine or backstitch by hand.

- Turn the garment inside out and fold the hem up ½ inch, tucking the raw edge over again so that it is safely inside the hem.

- Iron and pin the fabric, then sew using a straight stitch on a machine or backstitch by hand.

CARING FOR KITCHENWARE

Ruined kitchenware ruins dinners. But if you buy the right pieces and take care of them, this should be a very rare occurrence indeed.

Cast iron

Cast iron is one of the most durable materials when it comes to kitchenware, but it does need a bit of TLC to remain in tip-top condition.

Seasoning cast iron

Some pans come pre-seasoned, but if yours hasn't, then it's worth taking the time to season it properly before you start cooking up a storm. You can also use this method to restore rusty iron pans to their former glory.

- Scrub and sand off any rust; clean, and dry the pan.

- Take some avocado, canola, high-quality virgin oil, or 100 percent organic flaxseed oil (this isn't a cooking oil but is sold in health food stores as an omega-3 supplement) and wipe it on both the outside and inside of the pan.

- Wipe off the oil until only a very fine layer remains.

- Place the pan upside down in a cold oven (it's worth having foil or a tray below it to catch any drips) and bake at a high temperature (up to 500°F) for twenty minutes.

- Repeat the wipe-on, wipe-off, and bake process up to six times until the pan is gleaming and black. The natural nonstick surface you're left with will be worth it. (Don't be tempted to put on a thicker layer of oil, as it's likely to flake off during washing.)

The seasoning of a pan should get better over time and become more nonstick, especially if you oil the pan regularly or cook fatty foods. To avoid scratches, use wood, plastic, or silicone utensils. If you burn some sticky food onto the bottom of the pan, simply scrub it off and re-season the pan. One of the great things about cast iron is that there is no nonstick surface to erode. You can always take it back to the metal and start again. This is why these pans can last for centuries.

Washing cast iron

Wash the pan as soon as possible after cooking. Never put it in the dishwasher—I found this out the hard way! Also, never put a hot pan into cold water (or vice versa), because this can create cracks or cause the iron to warp.

One of the best ways to clean your pan is to simply boil a little water in it and gently wipe the surface with a cloth as the water is bubbling. Hold the cloth with tongs, so you don't burn yourself. This method doesn't even require soap. You can also wash cast iron with warm soapy water, but don't submerge the pan completely. Use a gentle implement (no wire wool or metal scrubbers) and wipe as gently as possible.

Dry the pan by tipping out the water and leaving it on the burner until the moisture has evaporated. For extra protection, give it a quick wipe with oil and leave it on the burner for another two minutes to keep the seasoning strong. It will smoke, but this is a sign that it is working.

Most important, your pans must be dried thoroughly. When you put them away, keep the lids off to prevent moisture in the atmosphere from rusting them. As a bit of an extra defense, you can place a cloth or teabag inside the pan to soak up moisture from the air.

Knives

A decent set of knives can be the difference between heaven and hell in the kitchen, so it's worth investing in a good set and keeping them in tip-top condition.

Using

Use knives for what they should be used for to prevent injury to the knife or yourself.

Washing

All knives should be washed and dried by hand; leaving them in a damp dishwasher will leave them more susceptible to rust and breakage.

If you do spot rust on stainless-steel knives, cutlery, or utensils, scrub it off gently without scratching the metal. Use a cleaner such as Bar Keepers Friend or a paste of lemon juice and cream of tartar. A layer of chromium oxide should form of its own accord in a few days.

Storing

Never dump knives in a drawer—the movement of the drawer causes them to rub together and dulls the blades, and you're more likely to cut yourself trying to get one out. I have a universal knife block that stores knives of any size, which I recommend, as it's more future-proof than a knife block designed only to take a particular brand.

To avoid rust caused by moisture, keep a moisture absorber such as silica gel or rock salt in the drawer with your stainless-steel cutlery and utensils.

Maintaining

Hone your knives (that aren't serrated) regularly. Make it a ritual of your Sunday meal perhaps. You'll need a honing steel to do this, which is at least as long as your longest knife. Run the blade against the honing rod at a twenty-degree angle. If you're unsure or feeling nervous, look up tutorials online for the proper technique. If you like, you can imagine you're Arya Stark while you're doing it.

Sharpen your knives once or twice a year with your own knife sharpener or by sending them to an expert.

Cutting boards

Never put a wood board in the dishwasher or leave it in the sink, as the water will make it warp and crack; a simple wipe-down with soapy water is all that is necessary. If you've been working with raw meat, you can add a little bleach if you want to take extra precautions. Dry it well before storing.

Oil your board every couple of months to prevent cracking. A food-grade mineral oil works best. First, make sure the board is especially clean and dry. Rub it gently with a cloth soaked in the oil, leave the oil on for a few hours or overnight, and then wipe off any excess stickiness. You can oil your wood spoons in the same way to prevent them from drying and splitting.

If you're using a plastic cutting board, there is no need to oil it. Just make sure it can withstand the dishwasher temperatures.

Pots and pans

You don't need an elaborate cookware set to produce delicious meals. If you stick to the basics you need to get the job done, you will save money, hassle, and kitchen storage.

Cooking

Make sure that you put your pans on the right-size burner so the flames don't burn the outside or melt the handles. Check the manufacturer's instructions to see what temperatures they can withstand.

Use plastic, wood, or silicone implements to keep your nonstick scratch-free.

Washing

Let pans cool before putting them in water. If a particularly stubborn meal is stuck to a pan, leave it to soak in hot soapy water until it softens. Then, use nylon scrubbers or natural bristle brushes to scrub it clean, as this will prevent scratches.

Steel and aluminum pans might do fine in a dishwasher (always check what the manufacturer says), but copper pots should be washed by hand. Steer clear of bleach, as it can cause pitting in copper pots.

To get stains out of nonstick pans, boil up a brew consisting of two parts water and one part liquid bleach with a couple of tablespoons baking soda. Five minutes of boiling should do the trick.

Storing

If you have space, hanging pans prevents the dents and scratches that occur by stacking them on shelves. Coat your nonstick pans with a very fine layer of cooking oil before putting them away, as this will increase the lifespan of the nonstick surface.

Polishing

Some people like to polish their copper pots to keep them bright. This can be nice aesthetically, but it isn't necessary for the longevity of the pots. Many professional chefs prefer to let their pans develop a natural patina over time.

Plastic and rubber implements

Make sure you have the right tools for the job you need to do. Know the limitations of your utensils, such as heat resistance, so your meal isn't ruined while you are still cooking it.

Using

Make sure that anything you put in the microwave is microwave-safe and that any plastics are not heated more than they can take.

Washing

Some plastics can react badly to the dishwasher. If in doubt, wash by hand. If your plastic storage containers get stained, a paste of baking soda and water will usually clean it.

Storing

If you have any plastic or rubber kitchen implements or storage boxes, be aware that sunlight and heat can degrade them, so keep them in a cool dry place. If you find any of your plastics become smelly, pop some newspaper in them to absorb the odors.

A note on heat-resistant glass

Borosilicate glass, used for French presses, measuring cups, and some glasses, is a super-durable material, but be sure never to pour boiling water into it, as it can explode. Wait until the water has cooled just a touch and then always use a wood spoon, never metal, to stir the liquid.

TROUBLESHOOTING HOME APPLIANCES

Appliances probably cause us more stress than all our other possessions put together. We can diminish this through buying well, but also by being savvy as to why they stop working to begin with. The first step is to be organized. Keep all your manuals and warranties together in a file. (I separate household appliances from personal electronics.) Keep any extra parts in a labeled box or bag. That way, when the appliance goes, the spare parts can go too (or you can donate or sell them), and you won't have any "mystery cables" cluttering up your house.

First defense

Many expensive repair calls are for something very simple. Save yourself money by working through this list before you call someone in to help.

- Has it overheated? Turn it off. Wait ten minutes and see if it will restart.

- Check the settings. Is a timer on by mistake? Or is it on a setting that undermines what you're trying to do? For example, in your espresso maker, leaving the steam wand turned on can stop the water from flowing through the coffee grounds.

- Check the power connections.

- Check if there is any regular maintenance that you haven't done. Dirty cooling coils are the cause of almost half the repairs for fridges, so give them a clean.

- Check the manual for troubleshooting.

- Check online to see if anyone else has had a similar problem and has a quick fix.

- Call customer service and ask for advice.

- Call your local repairman and ask for advice.

Appliance failure

Failure at the beginning of an appliance's life may be because of a fault that hasn't been picked up at the manufacturing stage or because it is being used incorrectly. If you've gone through all of the preceding troubleshooting advice and the appliance still isn't working, do the following.

- If it goes wrong within thirty days of purchase and it's a manufacturing fault, you can return it.

- If it's within warranty, the manufacturer should take responsibility for the repair. The retailer you bought it from may have an extended warranty or replacement policy from whom you can request a repair or return. The credit card you bought it on may offer insurance.

- If it's out of warranty, get a quote for the repair and parts.

- Check to see if you can get the parts cheaper elsewhere (make sure they are still reputable parts). Repair it yourself at a repair party or pay for the product to be fixed by a professional repairer.

MAINTAINING APPLIANCES

Even if you thoroughly researched and vetted your appliance purchases, wear and tear can cause problems to flare up. Take care of your machines so minor issues don't grow into big (and expensive) problems.

Clothes dryer

- Clean out the lint filter, heat exchangers, and sensors regularly (if your machine has them).

- Separate your clothes to stop them from balling in the machine, which leads to longer drying times.

- Don't overload the dryer.

- Always read the label on the clothes to ensure they can be tumble-dried.

Coffee maker

- Descale regularly (depending on how hard your water is).

- You can use a descaler or a half-and-half mixture of water and vinegar. Boil it up in the carafe, rinse it out, and repeat until the scale is gone.

Dishwasher

- Rinse your dishes before you put them in the dishwasher.

- Clean out the filter at least once a month.

- Run a cleaning cycle with a cup of vinegar on the top shelf or with dishwasher cleaner every six months.

- When stacking the dishwasher, make sure that nothing can snag on the spinning arms.

Garbage disposal

- Run cold water down with your food. This helps to solidify any fats, making them easier to chop and less likely to stick to the blades.

- Throw frozen vinegar cubes and chopped pieces of lemon into the disposal unit to clean the blades and freshen.

Microwave

- Clean any splatters as soon as they happen or they can get baked on and become notoriously difficult to remove.

Refrigerator

- The seals of the fridge can crack, causing air to get in. Be sure to wipe them clear of any grime, and add some petroleum jelly every six months to keep them supple.

- Clean the cooling coils (usually situated underneath or behind the fridge) every year, or every six months if you have pets. You can access them by taking off the kick plate or pulling the fridge out to get behind it. Vacuum up the dust and use a long, thin brush to sweep as much dust off the coils as possible. Doing this regularly can significantly increase your fridge's life.

Stove/Oven

- Clean the burners as you go along and do a thorough cleaning every two weeks.

- Avoid spraying cleaner into the burners, as this can affect the electrics.

- Use a drip pan underneath anything liable to splatter onto the floor of your oven and clean up spills as they happen.

Toaster

- Clean out the crumbs regularly and keep the filaments free of dust.

Washing machine

- Use the right settings for the clothes you have in the washer.

- Be sure nothing but fabric is going into the machine (check pockets for keys and other objects).

- Replace the fill hose roughly every five years.

- Do not overstuff the washing machine.

- Descale every 3 to 6 months depending on the hardness of your water.

APPENDIX II

Know Your Warranties

We've arrived at the sexiest part of this book! While research-ing products, I would spend an inordinate amount of time looking at the small print of warranties. Here's a simple breakdown so you know your "limited lifetimes" from your "full no quibbles."

First, always make sure you're clear on who is giving the warranty. Is it the retailer or the manufacturer? A warranty or a guarantee generally means almost the same thing and people use the terms interchangeably, although a guarantee might be more likely to include labor costs than a warranty, which might just cover the cost of parts. Bear in mind that many small companies might have excellent aftercare services and will do all they can to help you if you have an issue with their product, but they might not shout about having a warranty. So, if you like a product, give the company a call. Ask them what their policy would be if the product broke in various scenarios.

Full warranty/guarantee

If a product has a full warranty, then the manufacturer has committed to fix or replace it within the period specified. A full warranty can range from thirty days to life, but may exclude wear and tear.

Limited warranty/guarantee

Sometimes, a company puts certain limitations on the warranty. A common limitation is that they cover only manufacturing defects, so any accidental damage is not covered.

Lifetime warranties

Different companies have different definitions of what "lifetime" means. For some, they mean the lifetime of the original owner. Le Creuset has such a policy. For other companies, it is "the lifetime of the product" that they are warranting. This can mean the estimated amount of time that the product is expected to last (ask how long that is) or it could mean until the materials making up the product break down through normal use. Some companies misuse the term "lifetime warrantee" and ensure that as it comes with so many conditions, it is barely offering any coverage at all. If in doubt, check the small print. Or better yet, call and talk through what is and isn't covered.

Some warrantees are only valid if you keep up the maintenance of the product, such as servicing, so make sure to take note of what servicing is needed and add it to your yearly action list (see page 245).

A full, no-quibble lifetime warranty

This generally means that the company is prepared to take back the item at any stage and repair or replace it. These are the ones that we like the best at BuyMeOnce.

Endnotes

1 | MINDFUL CURATION

1. Tim Kasser, "Materialist Values and Goals," *Annual Review of Psychology*, 67 (2016), 489–514.

2. Cited in "Advertising's Toxic Effect on Eating and Body Image," Harvard School of Public Health, www.hsph. harvard.edu/news/features/advertisings-toxic-effect-on-eating-and-body-image.

3. Monika A. Bauer, James E. B. Wilkie, Jung K. Kim, and Galen V. Bodenhausen, "Cuing Consumerism: Situational Materialism Undermines Personal and Social Well-Being," *Psychological Sciences*, 23: 5 (2012), 517–24.

4. Rik Pieters, "Bidirectional Dynamics of Materialism and Loneliness: Not Just a Vicious Cycle," *Journal of Consumer Research*, 40: 4 (2013), 615–31.

5. Cited in L. Entis, "Chronic Loneliness Is a Modern-Day Epidemic," *Fortune* magazine, 22 June 2016, fortune. com/2016/06/22/loneliness-is-a-modern-day-epidemic/.

6. Jean M. Twenge, W. K. Campbell, and E. C. Freeman, "Generational Differences in Young Adults' Life Goals, Concern for Others, and Civic Orientation, 1966–2009," *Journal of Personality and Social Psychology*, 102 (2012), 1045–62.

7. University of Michigan, "Empathy: College students don't have as much as they used to, study finds," *ScienceDaily*, 29 May 2010.

8. Centers for Disease Control and Prevention figures, 2017.

9. *Meet the Natives*, Channel 4, UK, first broadcast 27 September 2007.

10. *Life Stripped Bare*, Channel 4, UK, first broadcast 5 July 2016.

11. Natasha Lekes, Nora H. Hope, Lucie Gouveia, Richard Koestner, and Frederick L. Philippe, "Influencing value priorities and increasing well-being: The effects of reflecting on intrinsic values," *Journal of Positive Psychology*, 7: 3 (2012), 249–61.

2 | PLANNED OBSOLESCENCE

1. Roy Sheldon and Egmont Arens, *Consumer Engineering: A New Technique for Prosperity* (Harper & Bros., 1932), 65.

2. Bernard London, "Ending the Depression through Planned Obsolescence" (1932), 5, catalog.hathitrust.org/Record/006829435.

3. *The Light Bulb Conspiracy*, Cosima Dannoritzer and Steve Michelson

4. (directors), RTVE, Televisión Española, 2010.

5. Scoping report, Environmental Resources Management Limited, February 2011.

6. www.which.co.uk/news/2015/06/are-washing-machines-built-to-fail-406177.

7. www.which.co.uk.

8. Brook Lyndhurst, Defra Research Project DE01-022: "Public understanding of product lifetimes and durability," 26 March 2010.

9. Tim Cooper, "Inadequate Life? Evidence of Consumer Attitudes to Product Obsolescence," *Journal of Consumer Policy*, 27 (2004), 421–49.

10. Nigel Whiteley, *Design for Society* (Reaktion Books, 1993).

11. Christine Frederick, *Selling Mrs. Consumer* (Business Bourse, 1929), 246.

12. Ibid.

13. C. Cole, T. Cooper, and A. Gnanapragasam, "Extending Product Lifetimes Through WEEE Reuse and Repair: Opportunities and Challenges in the UK," *Electronic Goes Green 2016+*, Nottingham Trent University, Nottingham, 2016.

14. "Waste statistics: electrical and electronic equipment," Eurostat Statistics Explained, European Union, 2017, ec.europa.eu/eurostat/statistics-explained/index.php/Waste_statistics_electrical_and_electronic_equipment.

15. Cole, Cooper, and Gnanapragasam, op. cit.

16. *What to Buy and Why*, 7 Wonder Productions, UK, first broadcast BBC, January–February 2016.

17. J. F. McCullough, "Design Review—Cars '59," *Industrial Design*, February 1959, 79.

18. Donald A. Norman, *The Design of Everyday Things* (Basic Books, 1988; revised edition MIT Press, 2013), 143.

3 | ADVERTISING

1. "Brooks Stevens Biography," Milwaukee Art Museum, 2017, mam.org/collection/archives/brooks/bio.php.

2. www.nielsen.com/content/dam/nielsenglobal/jp/docs/report/2014/Nielsen_Advertising_and_%20Audiences%20Report-FINAL.pdf.

3. Ibid.

4. Cited in Sheree Johnson, "New Research Sheds Light on Daily Ad Exposures," *SJ Insights*, 29 August 2014, sjinsights.net/2014/09/29/new-research-sheds-light-on-daily-ad-exposures.

5. "Kevin the Hamster," Levi's Original ad, first broadcast August 1998.

6. Cited in Luke Brynley-Jones, "Can online customer service deliver a higher ROI than marketing?" *Our Social Times: Social Media for Business*, 2016, oursocialtimes.com/can-customer-service-deliver-a-higher-roi-than-marketing.

7. www.medium.com/on-advertising/why-we-just-replaced-68-tube-adverts-with-cat-pictures-9ed1ae1177d0.

8. "Fifteen Million Merits," *Black Mirror*, Zeppotron for Channel 4, UK, first broadcast 11 December 2011.

4 | MARKETING

1. Rance Crain, "Viewpoint: Who knows what ads lurk in the hearts of consumers? The inner mind knows," *Ad Age*, 9 June 1997, adage.com/article/special-report-magazines-the-alist/viewpoint-ads-lurk-hearts-consumers-mind/71786/.

2. Matthew J. Baker and Lisa M. George, "The Role of Television in Household Debt: Evidence from the 1950s," *The B.E. Journal of Economic Analysis & Policy*, 10: 1 (Advances), Article 41 (2010); Stuart Fraser and David Paton, "Does Advertising Increase Labour Supply? Time series evidence from the UK," *Journal of Applied Economics*, 35 (2003), 1357–68; L. Golden, "A Brief History of Long Work Time and the Contemporary Sources of Overwork," *Journal of Business Ethics*, 84 (2009), 217–27.

3. www.theguardian.com/lifeandstyle/2011/feb/08/parents-and-parenting-disney-channel.

4. Juliet B. Schor, *Born to Buy: The Commercialized Child and the New Consumer Culture* (Scribner, 2004), 21.

5. J. McNeal and C. Yeh, "Born to Shop," *American Demographics*, June (1993), 34–9.

6. D. Hood, "Is Advertising to Kids Wrong? Marketers Respond," *Kidscreen*, 15 November 2000.

7. Brian L. Wilcox et al., Report of the APA Task Force on Advertising and Children, American Psychological Association, 20 February 2004, www.apa.org/pi/families/resources/advertising-children.pdf.

8. Raymond W. Preiss, ed., *Mass Media Effects Research: Advances Through Meta-Analysis* (Routledge, 2013).

9. J. L. Weicha, K. E. Peterson, D. S. Ludwig, et al., "When Children Eat What They Watch: Impact of Television Viewing on Dietary Intake in Youth," *Archives of Pediatric and Adolescent Medicine*, 60 (2006), 436–42.

10. Marvin E. Goldberg and Gerald J. Gorn, "Some Unintended Consequences of TV Advertising to Children," *Journal of Consumer Research*, 5: 1 (1978), 22–9.

11. Cai and Zhao, 2010, cited in "Advertising to Children and Teens: Current Practices," *Common Sense Media,* spring 2014, www.commonsensemedia.org/file/csm-advertisingresearch brief-20141pdf/download.

12. http://www.commercialfreechildhood.org/sites/default/files/babies.pdf.

13. marketinglaw.osborneclarke.com/retailing/colgates-80-of-dentists-recommend-claim-under-fire.

14. Bain & Company, Diamond Industry Report for Antwerp World Diamond Centre (AWDC), 2011.

15. Haribo, *Just Too Good*, Quiet Storm, 27 January 2012.

16. Niels Van de Ven Marcel Zeelenberg and Rik Pieters, "The Envy Premium in Product Evaluation," *Journal of Consumer Research*, 37: 6, 1 April 2011, 984–98, doi. org/10:1086/657239.

17. bgr.com/2015/06/17/samsung-advertising-fails-iphone.

18. Tatiana Pilieva, *First Kiss*, 10 March 2014, www.youtube .com/watch?v=IpbDHxCV29A.

19. Christie Barakat, "What Brands Can Learn from Wren's 'First Kiss,'" *Adweek*, 14 March 2014, www.adweek.com/digital/ brands-viral-video-wren-first-kiss.

20. Anne E. Becker et al., "Eating behaviors and attitudes following prolonged exposure to television among ethnic Fijian adolescent girls," *British Journal of Psychiatry*, 180: 6 (2002), 509–14.

21. Marisabel Romero and Adam W. Craig, "Costly Curves: How Human-Like Shapes Can Increase Spending," *Journal of Consumer Research*, 44: 1 (2017), 80–98.

22. adespresso.com/academy/blog/use-fomo-marketing-social-media.

23. www.linkedin.com/pulse/secret-science-fomo-marketing-advertising-joseph-j-sanchez.

24. www.jwt.com/blog/consumer_insights/got-social-media-fomo.

25. Thales S. Teixeira, "The Rising Cost of Consumer Attention: Why You Should Care, and What You Can Do about It," Harvard Business School Working Paper No. 14-055, January 2014, 6.

26. Cited in Stacy Conradt, "The stories behind 10 famous product placements," *The Week*, 11 December 2012, theweek.com/articles/469629/stories-behind-10-famous-product-placements.

27. TBrandStudio, "How Our Energy Needs Are Changing, in a Series of Interactive Charts," *The New York Times*, 2017, paidpost.nytimes.com/chevron/a-complex-flow-of-energy.html?_r=0#.WYN344X_QqZ.

28. www.coty.com/news/daisy-marc-jacobs-tweetshop-grabs-attention-industry, 8 May 2014.

29. J. Eighmey and S. Sar, "Harlow Gale and the Origins of the Psychology of Advertising," *Journal of Advertising,* 36: 4 (2007), 147–58.

30. "Consumer Neuroscience: Capture a more comprehensive view of the non-conscious aspects of consumer decision-making with the most complete set of neuroscience tools at a global scale," www.nielsen.com/uk/en/solutions/measurement/consumer-neuroscience.html.

5 | FASTER AND FASTER FASHION

1. Cited in Juliet Schor, *Plenitude: The New Economics of True Wealth* (Penguin, 2010).

2. Christ Celetti, "The Present and Future of Men's Fashion," *Ogilvy*, 18 February 2016, www.ogilvy.com/news-views/the-present-and-future-of-mens-fashion.

3. Nigel Whiteley, *Design for Society* (Reaktion Books, 1993).

4. D. Wilson et al., "Just think: The challenges of the disengaged mind," *Science*, 345: 6192 (2014), 75–7.

5. Mary Quant, *Quant on Quant* (Cassell, 1966; V&A Publishing, 2012), 74.

6. Maya Oppenheim, "YouTube star Zoella reportedly earns at least £50,000 a month according to newly released accounts," *Independent*, 13 March 2016, www.independent.co.uk/news/people/ zoella-youtube-earnings-50000-sunday-times-alfie-deyes-a6928666.html.

7. www.youtube.com/watch?v=tOafTz1RgXA.

8. www.greenpeace.org/international/Global/international/briefings/toxics/2016/Fact-Sheet-Timeout-for-fast-fashion.pdf.

9. *Sweatshop: Deadly Fashion*, Aftenposten, Norway, first broadcast April 2014.

10. Carbon Trust (2011).

11. Caitlin Moran, *How to Be a Woman* (Ebury Press, 2012), 211.

12. Karen J. Pine, *Mind What You Wear: The Psychology of Fashion* (Amazon Media, 2014), 65 and 115.

13. Ibid, 365.

6 | BORN TO SHOP

1. www.theatlantic.com/technology/archive/2012/04/the-100-year-march-of-technology-in-1-graph/255573.

2. "Latest trend sweeping China: Lighter skin," *CBS News*, 14 October 2012, www.cbsnews.com/news/latest-trend-sweeping-china-lighter-skin.

3. Karli K. Watson, "Visual Preferences for Sex and Status in Female Rhesus Macaques," *Journal of Animal Cognition*, 15: 3 (2012), 401–407.

4. Cited in Geoffrey Miller, *Must-Have: The Hidden Instincts Behind Everything We Buy* (Vintage, 2010), 13.

5. Ibid., 83.

6. Quoted in "Bonfire of fashion's vanities," *Evening Standard*, 1 February 2010, www.standard.co.uk/lifestyle/bonfire-of-fashions-vanities-6743489.html.

7. www.theguardian.com/uk/2004/jun/09/britishidentity/features11.

7 | BECOMING A CURATOR

1. Christine Frederick, *Selling Mrs. Consumer* (Business Bourse, 1929), 326.

2. Thomas N. Robinson et al., "Effects of Fast Food Branding on Young Children's Taste Preferences," *Archive of Pediatrics and Adolescent Medicine Journal*, 161: 8 (2007), 792–7.

3. T. Langer et al., "Is It Really Love? A Comparative Investigation of the Emotional Nature of Brand and Interpersonal Love," *Psychology and Marketing*, 32: 6 (2015), 624–34.

8 | TAKING STOCK

1. Evan Zislis, *ClutterFree Revolution* (Juniper Press, 2015), 52.

9 | BEFORE YOU SHOP

1. www.statisticbrain.com/average-daily-activities.

2. W. Mischel, *The Marshmallow Test: Mastering Self-Control* (Little, Brown and Company, 2014).

3. www.bloomberg.com/news/articles/2013-03-21/shoppers-mobile-blinders-force-checkout-aisle-changes.

4. Charles Duhigg, *The Power of Habit: Why We Do What We Do in Life and Business* (Random House, 2012).

5. *Ann Widdecombe to the Rescue*, BBC Two, first broadcast 28 June 2005.

6. www.baylor.edu/mediacommunications/news. php?action=story&story=176436.

10 | OUT AT THE SHOPS

1. Eve Reid, "Silent selling: the art and science of visual merchandising," Hospice UK Retail Conference 2016, www.youtube.com/watch?v=ICViBwGb—4.

2. Ibid.

3. Eric R. Spangenberg, et al., "Gender-congruent ambient scent influences on approach and avoidance behaviors in a retail store," *Journal of Business Research*, 59: 12 (2006), 1281–7, www.sciencedirect.com/science/article/pii/S0148296306001299.

4. Charles Duhigg, "How Companies Learn Your Secrets," *The New York Times* magazine, 16 February 2012, www.nytimes.com/2012/02/19/magazine/shopping-habits .html?_r=1&hp=&pagewanted=all.

5. Annina Claesson, "Using Gamification on Your Online Community Platform: Principles, Examples, and Ideas," *VeryConnect*, 28 February 2017, www.veryconnect.com/ blog/using-gamification-on-your-online-community-platform-principles-examples-and-ideas.

6. www.statista.com/statistics/194424/amount-spent-on-toys-per-child-by-country-since-2009.

11 | THE BUYMEONCE BUYING GUIDE

1. Cited in Rachel Botsman and Roo Rogers, *What's Mine Is Yours: The Rise of Collaborative Consumption* (HarperCollins, 2010).

2. www.which.co.uk/reviews/fridge-freezers/article/which-fridge-freezer-brand/most-reliable-fridge-freezer-brands.

3. www.which.co.uk/reviews/vacuum-cleaners/article/which-vacuum-cleaner-brand/most-reliable-vacuum-cleaner-brands.

4. nrf.com/media/press-releases/halloween-spending-reach-84-billion-highest-survey-history.

5. www.yahoo.com/beauty/this-is-how-much-time-the-average-person-spends-214856853.html.

6. www.dailymail.co.uk/femail/article-3211309/Women-spend-TWO-YEARS-life-applying-make-splashing-12-000-cosmetics.html.

7. www.dailymail.co.uk/femail/article-2188742/How-modern-parents-childrens-demands-buy-latest-toys-gadgets.html.

8. UCLA, "A Cluttered Life: Middle-Class Abundance," episode 1 premiere date: 23 December 2013.

9. www.independent.co.uk/news/education/education-news/the-nursery-that-took-all-the-childrens-toys-away-1125048.html.

12 | KEEPING AND CARING

1. Cited in Saleem Ahmad et al., "How Does Matter Lost and Misplace Items Issue and Its Technological Solutions in 2015: A Review Study," *IOSR Journal of Business and Management*, 17: 4 (2015), 79–84.

2. Cited in "Smartphone thefts drop as kill switch usage grows, but Android users are still waiting for the technology," *Consumer Reports*, 11 June 2015, www.consumerreports.org/cro/news/2015/06/smartphone-thefts-on-the-decline/index.htm.

13 | ON MONEY AND HAPPINESS

1. Helga Dittmar, *Consumer Culture, Identity and Well-being: The search for the "good life" and the "body perfect"* (Psychology Press, 2007).

2. www.apa.org/news/press/releases/stress/2014/stress-report.pdf.

3. www.jamesaltucher.com/2011/01/what-it-feels-like-to-be-rich.

4. "Warren Buffet," *Forbes*, 2017, www.forbes.com/profile/warren-buffett.

5. "Warren Buffet: his best quotes," *Telegraph*, 14 February 2012, www.telegraph.co.uk/finance/newsbysector/banksandfinance/8381363/Warren-Buffett-his-best-quotes.html.

6. Morris Altman, *Handbook of Contemporary Behavioral Economics: Foundations and developments* (M. E. Sharpe, 2006).

7. www.researchgate.net/publication/236848002_The_relationship_of_materialism_to_debt_and_financial_well-being_The_case_of_Iceland's_perceived_prosperity.

8. Global umbrella survey results, Sunnycomb Tumblr, 1 July 2014, sunnycomb.tumblr.com/post/90373669845/global-umbrella-survey-results.

9. www.huffingtonpost.com/2013/05/23/retail-therapy-shopping_n_3324972.html.

10. Viktor E. Frankl, *Man's Search for Meaning* (Verlag für Jugend und Volk, 1946; Simon & Schuster, 1963; Rider, 2004). 104 (1963 ed.).

11. Cited by Robert Waldringer, "What makes a good life? Lessons from the longest study on happiness," TED talk, November 2015.

12. Ibid.

13. Arthur Aron, et al., "The Experimental Generation of Interpersonal Closeness: A Procedure and Some Preliminary Findings," *Personality and Social Psychology Bulletin*, 23: 4 (1997), 363–77, journals.sagepub.com/doi/pdf/10:1177/0146167297234003.

14. David Marjoribanks and Anna Darnell Bradley, *You're not alone: the quality of the UK's social relationships* (Relate, 2017), 14.

15. Ethan Kross, et al., "Facebook Use Predicts Decline in Subjective Well-Being in Young Adults," *PLOS: One*, 14 August 2013.

16. www.hbs.edu/faculty/Publication%20Files/10-012.pdf.

17. ggsc-web02.ist.berkeley.edu/images/application_uploads/norton-spendingmoney.pdf.

18. James Wallman, *Stuffocation: Living more with less* (Crux Publishing, 2013).

19. A. Kumar, et al., "Waiting for Merlot: Anticipatory Consumption of Experiential and Material Purchases," *Psychological Science*, 25: 10 (2014), 1924–31.

CONCLUSION

1. Victor Papanek, *Design for the Real World: Human Ecology and Social Change* (Academy Chicago Publishers, 1971, 1985).

2. Bill Watterson, "Some Thoughts on the Real World by One Who Glimpsed It and Fled" speech given at Kenyon College, Gambier, Ohio, 20 May 1990, web.mit.edu/jmorzins/www/C-H-speech.html.

3. www.footprintnetwork.org.

4. earthobservatory.nasa.gov/Features/WorldOfChange/
   decadaltemp.php.

5. Quoted in Andrew Simms, "A cat in hell's chance—why
   we're losing the battle to keep global warming below 2C,"
   The Guardian, 19 January 2017, www.theguardian.com/
   environment/2017/jan/19/cat-in-hells-chance-why-losing-
   battle-keep-global-warming-2c-climate-change.

6. www.nationalgeographic.com/magazine/2013/09/rising-seas-
   ice-melt-new-shoreline-maps.

7. Simms, op. cit.

8. www.theguardian.com/environment/2015/dec/02/
   worlds-richest-10-produce-half-of-global-carbon-emissions-
   says-oxfam.

Further Reading

Altman, Morris, *Handbook of Contemporary Behavioral Economics: Foundations and Developments* (M. E. Sharpe, 2006).

Botsman, Rachel, and Roo Rogers, *What's Mine Is Yours: The Rise of Collaborative Consumption* (HarperCollins, 2010).

Brotheridge, Chloë, *The Anxiety Solution: A Quieter Mind, a Calmer You* (Michael Joseph, 2017).

Brown, Derren, *Happy: Why More or Less Everything Is Absolutely Fine* (Bantam Press, 2016).

Butlin, John, *Product Durability and Product Life Extension: Their Contribution to Solid Waste Management* (OECD, 1982).

Dittmar, Helga, *Consumer Culture, Identity, and Well-Being: The Search for the "Good Life" and the "Body Perfect"* (Psychology Press, 2007).

Duhigg, Charles, *The Power of Habit: Why We Do What We Do in Life and Business* (Random House, 2012).

Frankl, Viktor E., *Man's Search for Meaning* (Verlag für Jugend und Volk, 1946; Beacon Press, 1959; Rider, 2004).

Frederick, Christine, *Selling Mrs. Consumer* (Business Bourse, 1929).

Gilbert, Elizabeth, *Big Magic: Creative Living Beyond Fear* (Bloomsbury, 2016).

Gladwell, Malcolm, *Blink: The Power of Thinking without Thinking* (Little, Brown, 2005).

Jackson, Tim, *Prosperity without Growth: Economics for a Finite Planet* (Earthscan, 2009).

James, Oliver, *Affluenza* (Vermilion, 2007).

Lingerfelt, James Russell, *The Mason Jar* (William and Keats, 2014).

Lippincott, J. Gordon, *Design for Business* (Paul Theobald, 1947).

Midler, Paul, *Poorly Made in China: An Insider's Account of the Production Game* (John Wiley & Sons, 2009).

Miller, Geoffrey, *Must-Have: The Hidden Instincts Behind Everything We Buy* (Vintage, 2010).

Moran, Caitlin, *How to Be a Woman* (Ebury Press, 2012).

Papanek, Victor, *Design for the Real World: Human Ecology and Social Change (Chicago Review Press, 2005).*

Pine, Karen J., *Mind What You Wear: The Psychology of Fashion* (Amazon Media, 2014).

Preiss, Raymond W., ed., *Mass Media Effects Research: Advances Through Meta-Analysis* (Routledge, 2013).

Quant, Mary, *Quant on Quant* (Cassell, 1966; V&A Publishing, 2012).

Rubin, Gretchen, *The Happiness Project* (HarperCollins, 2009).

Schor, Juliet B., *Born to Buy: The Commercialized Child and the New Consumer Culture* (Scribner, 2004).

Sheldon, Roy, and Egmont Arens, *Consumer Engineering: A New Technique for Prosperity* (Harper & Bros., 1932).

Wallman, James, *Stuffocation: Living More with Less* (Crux Publishing, 2013).

Whiteley, Nigel, *Design for Society* (Reaktion Books, 1993).

Zislis, Evan, *ClutterFree Revolution* (Juniper Press, 2015).

Acknowledgments

It takes a village to birth a book, so I'm about to thank a village-worth of people for being the best midwives, consultant specialists, and book-sitters.

Huge thanks to Esmond Harmsworth for coming to me with the seed of an idea that it might be worth writing down the BuyMeOnce philosophy and tirelessly helping me through the process. Also to Kelly Snowden of Ten Speed Press for your faith and understanding and your enthusiasm for bringing the book to America.

There were many people generous enough with their time and expertise to add the threads of their thoughts into the tapestry of the book. Theo Davis for his insights into the mind of a salesman and for the eighteen hours he spent dreading my hair in university, only for me to decide dreadlocks weren't really me. It was an excellent lesson in self-knowledge. Lynne Drummond for squeezing me into her schedule (before her vacation) to be interviewed about the complexities of hoarding. My darling sister Juliet for all her brain-picking on how to purchase for a BuyMeOnce baby. You are a real inspiration. One day I'll be able to pack as lightly as you do. Tom Lawton and the engineers in various fields who have taken the time to talk me through the challenges they face and some of the misbehavior their industries are perpetuating. Thor Johnsen for letting me pump him for information on the world of big business, for being so candid, and for being one of the good guys. Helen Craven and Chloë Brotheridge for their wonderful hypnotherapy insights. Ben Shires for being so determinedly himself and being my style inspiration. Geoffrey Miller, first for writing the excellent book *Must-Have*, which was so engaging and made sense of so many of our strange buying habits, and also for being so sweet and encouraging when we met in Cambridge being "disruptors." Tim Cooper and Christine Cole at PLATE (Product Lifetimes and the Environment) for their encouragement and helpful answers to random questions. Jeremy of excellent beard fame, who was my research guru at the British Library, you always found just what I needed and always found a way to get it to me. Granny Ruth, for endlessly fascinating stories of how the world used to be. Please do keep writing in and letting us know your thoughts.

Only a few people saw the book before publication, but everyone who did helped to make it better. Laura Mucha, my brilliant book buddy, helped me make sense of my own thoughts, kept me semi-sane by getting me dancing on a roof in Turkey, and willed me on through sheer personality. I'm not sure the book would have got finished without you. Amanda Saxby, you were on the front line of my dyslexic grammar, meandering thought trains, leaps of logic, and rambling asides. My best maids, Tasmina Hoque and Clara Courtauld, for being encouraging and insightful early readers, and Helena for providing me with two of my most extravagant overspend anecdotes. Sally Nicholls and Marianne Power for being such wonderful literary sounding boards and answering panicked emails about blurbs, voice, and dastardly deadlines. Caitlin Moran for tweeted encouragement and allowing me to use your words on the cover. In fact, thank you for all your words and the wit and wisdom I have absorbed from them over the years. To the Creative Writing for Young People course at Bath Spa, especially Julia Green and Nicola Davies, this is not a children's book, but it wouldn't have been written half as well if it hadn't been for some of the foundations of the writing craft that were instilled in me by your teaching. Evan Zislis for being so generous with advice and endless enthusiasm on his mission to declutter the planet. Jonathan Wise for opening my eyes to the urgency of the situation we face. To all the great brands and companies who are showing the world that it's possible to be planet- and people-friendly and still turn a profit. You are the ones who will turn things around.

None of this book would have been possible if I hadn't been able to completely rely on the core BuyMeOnce team to carry on being brilliant while I sat in my shed writing. To the amazing, irrepressible, and irreplaceable Lily, James, Amanda, and Joe—thank you. Also thanks to Lucy Robinson for unfailing cheer and PR wizardry.

Finally, to my tribe. To Mark for being my first and most encouraging reader and making the whole BuyMeOnce dream a reality. To Mummy, Daddy, Jules, Kir, and all my lovely Buttons, Hayes, Milligans, and Taskers for the support and love that is so palpable, even when it comes from across oceans. To clan Cohen, especially Barbara, for welcoming me into your wonderfully vibrant family. Prim girl, you helped more than you'll ever know. Keep being you.

And especially to my darling Howard, who had to plan our wedding and cook dinner while his future wife became increasingly nocturnal and frazzled as deadlines approached. Thank goodness for you. I love you.

Index

Copyright © 2018 by Tara Button
Cover photograph © Shutterstock.com

All rights reserved.
Published in the United States by Ten Speed Press,
an imprint of the Crown Publishing Group, a division
of Penguin Random House LLC, New York.
www.crownpublishing.com
www.tenspeed.com

Ten Speed Press and the Ten Speed Press colophon are
registered trademarks of Penguin Random House LLC.

Originally published in paperback in Great Britain by Thorsons,
an imprint of HarperCollins Publishers, London, in 2018.

Library of Congress Cataloging-in-Publication Data
    Names: Button, Tara, author.
    Title: A life less throwaway : the lost art of buying for life /
    Tara Button.
    Description: First edition. | New York : Ten Speed Press, [2018]
    Identifiers: LCCN 2018011115
    Subjects: LCSH: Simplicity. | Consumer behavior. |
    Consumer education. | Quality of products.
    Classification: LCC BJ1496 .B89 2018 | DDC 381.3/3—dc23

Trade Paperback ISBN: 978-0-399-58251-6
eBook ISBN: 978-0-399-58252-3

Printed in the United States of America

Cover design by Steve Leard

10 9 8 7 6 5 4 3 2 1

First United States Edition